TOWARDS THE DEFINITION OF PHILOSOPHY

1. The Idea of Philosophy and the Problem of Worldview
2. Phenomenology and Transcendental Philosophy of Value

Martin Heidegger

With a Transcript of the Lecture-Course 'On the Nature of the University and Academic Study'

(Freiburg Lecture-Courses 1919)

Translated by Ted Sadler

continuum

Continuum

The Tower Building   80 Maiden Lane
11 York Road   Suite 704
London SE1 7NX   New York NY 10038

www.continuumbooks.com

© The Athlone Press 2000
This edition © 2008

Originally published in Germany as *Zur Bestimmung der Philosophie*
© Vittorio Klostermann GmbH, Frankfurt am Main, 1987

'Die Herausgabe dieses Werkes wurde aus Mitteln von
INTER NATIONES, Bonn gefördert'.

British Library Cataloguing in Publication Data
A catalogue record for this book is available from the British Library

Library of Congress Cataloging-in-Publication Data
A catalog record for this book is available from the Library of Congress.

ISBN 1-8470-6304-7 PB
ISBN 978-1-8470-6304-5

Typeset by RefineCatch Limited, Bungay, Suffolk
Printed and bound in Great Britain by
MPG Books Ltd, Bodmin, Cornwall

Contents

CHAPTER TWO

Critique of Teleological-Critical Method

PART TWO

PHENOMENOLOGY AS PRE-THEORETICAL PRIMORDIAL SCIENCE

CHAPTER ONE

Analysis of the Structure of Experience

CHAPTER TWO

The Problem of Presuppositions

CHAPTER THREE

Primordial Science as Pre-Theoretical Science

II PHENOMENOLOGY AND
TRANSCENDENTAL PHILOSOPHY OF VALUE

Summer Semester 1919

INTRODUCTION

PART ONE

HISTORICAL PRESENTATION OF THE PROBLEM

CHAPTER ONE

CHAPTER TWO

Translator's Foreword

This book is a translation of *Zur Bestimmung der Philosophie*, first published in 1987 as Volume 56/57 of Martin Heidegger's *Gesamtausgabe*. The two lecture-courses it contains were delivered by Heidegger at the University of Freiburg in 1919. They are the earliest extant lecture-courses by Heidegger, being given soon after he transferred from the theological to the philosophical faculty. The first course in particular, 'The Idea of Philosophy and the Problem of Worldview', is of great importance for its anticipation of ideas that find more complete expression in *Being and Time*, published in 1927. The second course, 'Phenomenology and Transcendental Philosophy of Value', provides a critical survey of the Neo-Kantianism which at that time was dominant in German universities. As in the second German edition (1999), the translation includes two appendices, 'On the Nature of the University and Academic Study', being an incomplete transcript from Oskar Becker of a lecture-course by Heidegger dating from the same period and addressing similar material to the other courses, and an excerpt from Franz-Joseph Brecht's transcript of the first lecture-course 'The Idea of Philosophy'.

Heidegger did not prepare these lecture-courses for publication, and my translation does not attempt to hide the unpolished and often conversational character of the German text. Some parts of the text, particularly in the second lecture-course, are in the nature of notes or reminders. In general I have striven for a maximally literal English rendering consistent with readability. Sometimes the original German of operational philosophical terms has been placed in square brackets within the text, and I have also provided a brief glossary. Books and articles referred to by

Heidegger have been translated in the text, their German titles being given in the footnotes. Further information on the origin of this volume can be found in the German Editor's Afterword.

For valuable assistance in the preparation of this translation I would like to thank Dr Ian Lyne of the University of Durham and the editors of Continuum Press.

Ted Sadler

Publisher's Note

The page numbering of the second German edition of 1999 has been retained within square brackets, enabling readers to refer, page by page, between this translation and the original text.

The Idea of Philosophy and the Problem of Worldview [1]

War Emergency Semester 1919

Preliminary Remarks [3]

Science and University Reform

The problem to whose scientific delineation, development and partial solution this lecture-course is dedicated, will reveal, in an increasingly radical and decisive manner, the following preparatory remarks to be incongruent and foreign.

The scientific idea to be pursued is such that with the achievement of a genuine methodological orientation we step out beyond and away from ourselves, and must methodologically remain behind in the sphere which is forever foreign to the most proper problematic of the science to be founded.

This modifying infringement, reform and even exclusion of the naive consciousness of immediate life is nothing accidental, resting on some arbitrarily chosen construction, on the organization of the lecture-course, or on a so-called philosophical 'standpoint'. It will rather prove itself a *necessity*, grounded in the essential matter of the problem and demanded by the specific nature of the problematic's scientific domain.

The idea of science therefore – and every element of its genuine realization – means a transforming intervention in the immediate consciousness of life; it involves a transition to a new attitude of consciousness, and thus its own form of the movement of spiritual life.

Only in philosophy as primordial science [*Urwissenschaft*] does this intervention of the idea of science into the context of natural life-consciousness occur in a primordial and radical sense. [4] But it can also be found in every genuine science in a derivative way, corresponding to its specific cognitive goals and methodological constitution.

The particular problematic of a science corresponds to a particular type of context of consciousness [*Bewußtseinszusammenhang*]. Its essential lawfulness can come to rule a consciousness. This expresses itself in ever purer form as a specific motivational context. In this way science becomes the habitus of a personal existence.

Every personal life has in all moments within its particular predominant life-world a relationship to that world, to the motivational values of the environing world, of the things of its life-horizon, of other human beings, of society. These life-relations can be pervaded – in quite diverse ways – by a genuine form of accomplishment and life-form, e.g. the scientific, religious, artistic, political.

The scientific man, however, does not stand in isolation. He is connected to a community of similarly striving researchers with its rich relations to students. The life-context of scientific consciousness expresses itself objectively in the formation and organization of scientific academies and universities.

The much discussed university reform is totally misguided, and is a total misunderstanding of all genuine revolutionizing of the spirit, when it now broadens its activities into appeals, protest meetings, programmes, orders and alliances: means that are antagonistic to the mind and serve ephemeral ends.

We are not yet ripe for *genuine* reforms in the university. Becoming ripe for them is the task of a *whole generation*. The renewal of the university means a rebirth of the genuine scientific consciousness and life-contexts. [5] But life-relations renew themselves only by returning to the genuine origins of the spirit. As historical phenomena they need the peace and security of genetic consolidation, in other words, the inner truthfulness of a worthwhile, self-cultivating life. Only life, not the noise of frenetic cultural programmes, is 'epoch-making'. Just as the 'active spirit' of literary novices is a hindering force, so also is the attempt, to be found everywhere in the special sciences (from biology to the history of literature and art), to summon up a scientific 'worldview' through the phraseological grammar of a corrupted philosophy.

But just as the awe of the religious man makes him silent in the face of his ultimate mystery, just as the genuine artist lives only in his work and detests all art-chatter, so the scientific man is effective only by way of the vitality of genuine research.

The awakening and heightening of the life-context of scientific consciousness is not the object of theoretical representation, but of exemplary pre-*living* [*Vorleben*] – not the object of practical provision of rules, but the effect of primordially motivated personal and non-personal *Being*. Only in this way are the life-world and life-type of science built up. Within this there is formed: science as genuine archontic life-form (i.e. the type of the researcher who lives absolutely in the pertinent content and origins of his problematic) and science as co-ruling habitual element in non-scientific life-worlds (type of the scientifically educated practical professional man, in whose life science retains its own ineradicable significance). Two outgrowths of scientific consciousness, which are only authentically realized where they grow from an inner calling. 'Man, be essential!' (Angelus Silesius) – 'Let those accept it who can' (Matthew 19: 12).

[6] The scientific demand for *methodological* development of problems poses the task of a *preliminary explication of the genuine problem*.

This includes an analysis that clears away crude and continually disruptive misunderstandings and naive preconceptions. We thus gain the essential direction for our treatment of the genuine problem; the individual steps of thought and the stages of problem-analysis become visible in their methodological teleology.

§ 1. Philosophy and Worldview

a) Worldview as Immanent Task of Philosophy

[7] Upon first attempting to understand the topic before us, one might almost be surprised at its triviality, excusing it as suitable material for one of those popular general educational courses given from time to time. One has at one's disposal a more or less clear conception of philosophy, especially in the present day, where philosophy, and speaking and writing about it, practically belongs to good form. Today, worldview is a spiritual concern of everyone: the peasant in the Black Forest has his worldview, consisting in the doctrinal content of his confession; the factory worker has his worldview, whose essence, perhaps, consists in regarding all religion as a superseded affair; certainly the so-called educated person has his worldview; the political parties have their worldviews. One hears nowadays about the antagonism between the Anglo-American and German worldviews.

If one strives for a higher autonomous worldview, cultivating a thinking free from religious and other dogmas, then one is doing philosophy. Philosophers bear the honourable title of 'great thinkers' in an exemplary sense. They are regarded as 'great' not only on account of the acuity and consistency of their thought, but even more because of its breadth and depth. They experience and view the world with heightened inner vitality, penetrating to its final sense or origin; they recognize nature as a cosmos of the ultimate lawfulness of simple movements [8] or energies.

Due to their broad knowledge of the particular sciences, of artistic-literary and political-social life, the philosophers gain an ultimate understanding of these spiritual worlds. Some solve the ultimate problems by remaining within a dualism of nature and spirit, others trace these two worlds back to one common origin – God – which is itself conceived *extra mundum* or made identical with all Being. Others interpret everything spiritual as natural, mechanical, energetic Being; still others, by contrast, treat all nature as spirit.

Within and by means of such fundamental conceptions of the world, man acquires the 'explanations' and interpretations of his individual and social life. The meaning and purpose of human existence, and of human creation as culture, are discovered.

In other words: the efforts of the great philosophers are directed towards what is in every sense ultimate, universal, and of universal validity. The inner struggle with the puzzles of life and the world seeks to come to rest by establishing the ultimate nature of these. Objectively stated: every great philosophy realizes itself in a worldview – every philosophy is, where its innermost tendency comes to unrestricted expression, metaphysics.

The formulation of our topic has received an unambiguous sense; we understand the meaning of the 'and' in our course title: this says more than an empty juxtaposition of philosophy and the problem of worldview. According to the previous analysis, the 'and' brings world-view and philosophy into the essential relation of their own task – of their nature. Philosophy and worldview mean essentially the same thing, but worldview brings the nature and task of philosophy more clearly to expression. *Worldview as the task of philosophy*: *therefore* a historical consideration of the manner in which philosophy performs this task.

b) Worldview as Limit of the Critical Science of Value [9]

Or is a quite different, critical, scientific conception of our topic still possible? If one reflects upon the fact that contemporary theory of knowledge, in so far as it does not, linking up with Aristotle, subscribe to a naive critical realism, stands decisively in the after-effect or renewal of Kant, then the hope for a metaphysics in the old sense will be essentially diminished: an experientially transcendent knowledge of super-sensible realities, forces, causes, is regarded as impossible.

Philosophy receives a scientific foundation in critical epistemology, upon whose fundamental insights the remaining philosophical disciplines – ethics, aesthetics, philosophy of religion – build. In all these disciplines – and in logic itself – 'critical' reflection leads back to ultimate values and absolute validities, whose totality can be brought into an ordered systematic coherence.

The system of values provides for the first time the scientific means for constructing a critical scientific worldview. This conception of philosophy stands in sharp contrast to every kind of uncritical speculation and constructive monism. It creates the scientifically elaborated foundation upon which a possible scientific worldview can arise, a worldview which seeks to be nothing other than the interpretation of the meaning of human existence and culture in respect of the system of those absolutely valid norms which in the course of human development have expressed themselves as the values of the true, the good, the beautiful and the holy.

Holding strictly to epistemological criticism, philosophy remains within the realm of consciousness, to whose three basic kinds of activity – thinking, willing and feeling – there correspond the logical, ethical and aesthetic [10] values which in their harmony coalesce into the value of the holy, the religious value. Here also philosophy culminates in a worldview, but one which is critical and scientific. The formation of such a worldview is admittedly also a matter of the personal stance of the philosopher towards life, the world and history. But this stance assumes norms through the results of scientific philosophy, where the personal stance of the philosopher must be – as in every science – excluded.

Worldview is not conceived here as actually identical with the task of scientific philosophy. As the science of value, the task of scientific philosophy is the system of values, and worldview stands right at the limit of philosophy – the two, however, come into a certain unity within the personality of the philosopher.

Thus we have come to a significantly more useful and superior interpretation of our topic: worldview as the limit of scientific philosophy, or scientific philosophy, i.e. the critical science of value, as the necessary foundation of a critical scientific worldview.

Through the *comparison* of the two conceptions of our topic, and through consideration of its historical expressions, we see that the problem of worldview is somehow connected with philosophy: in the *first case* worldview is defined as the *immanent task* of philosophy, that is, philosophy as in the final analysis *identical* with the teaching of a world-view; in the *other case* worldview is the *limit* of philosophy. Philosophy as critical science is *not identical* with the teaching of a worldview.

c) The Paradox of the Problem of Worldview. Incompatibility between Philosophy and Worldview [11]

The *critical* decision between the two conceptions of our topic readily suggests itself. Without at the moment entering into involved discussions, it is clear that the modern critical consciousness will decide for the second, scientific standpoint, and, as the most influential schools of contemporary philosophy testify, has already thus decided.

This preliminary explication of the possible conceptions of our topic guides us into a proper analysis of the problem. However, the precision and completeness of method demand that we first consider a formal question, namely whether all possible conceptions of our topic have been exhausted by the two formulations already canvassed.

The history of philosophy shows that, however diverse its forms may be, philosophy always has a connection with the question of worldview. Different possible conceptions of this topic arise only in regard to how they are connected. That is, despite all individual differences as to whether philosophy and worldview are identical or non-identical, *a connection exists*.

There remains only the empty possibility that no connection exists between the two, in which case worldview would be an utterly hetero-geneous structure to philosophy. Such a radical separation would contradict all previous conceptions of philosophy, for it would imply an entirely new concept of philosophy which would be totally unrelated to all the ultimate questions of humankind. Philosophy would thus be deprived of its most traditional entitlements as a regal, superior occupation. What value at all could it have if it should lose this role?

[12] If we recall the previously discussed conceptions, philosophy could no longer seriously come into consideration as science, for scientific philosophy, as the critical science of values founded on basic acts and norms of consciousness, has in its system an ultimate and necessary ten-dency towards a worldview.

We speak therefore of a paradox which apparently possesses a formal and methodological justification, but which also has the dubious distinction of leading to the disaster of all previous philosophy. This paradox, however, is our genuine problem. Thereby the two initially mentioned conceptions of our topic will be placed radically in question.

The expression 'problem of worldview' now receives a new meaning. Should it be shown that the construction of a worldview in no way belongs to philosophy, not even as a boundary task, and that it is a phenomenon foreign to philosophy, then such a demonstration would include showing the completely different character of 'worldview', that is, of *worldview in general and as such* – not this or that definite one. *The essence of worldview becomes a problem*, and indeed with respect to its interpretation from an overarching context of meaning.

The genuinely unphilosophical character of worldview can emerge only when it is set over against philosophy, and then only through the methodological tools of philosophy itself. Worldview becomes the *problem of philosophy* in a quite new sense. But the core of the problem lies in philosophy itself – it is itself a problem. The cardinal question concerns the nature and concept of philosophy. But the topic is formulated as '*the idea* of philosophy', more precisely 'the idea of philosophy as primordial science'.

PART ONE [13]

The Idea of Philosophy as Primordial Science

CHAPTER ONE
The Search for a Methodological Way

§ 2. The Idea of Primordial Science

a) Idea as Definite Determination

In philosophical usage, the word 'idea' has various meanings, which change according to system and 'standpoint' and so to some degree diverge. But from the history of the concept we can show, albeit with some forcing, a certain vague constant (common) content.

In its pre-philosophical employment, the word can mean something like 'dark image', 'foggy presentiment', a thought that has not been brought to clarity; there is no certainty in respect of the object intended by the idea, no grounded, unambiguous knowledge of its substantive content.

The word 'idea' has acquired a distinctive meaning in Kant's *Critique of Pure Reason*, a meaning which, in what follows, we shall again take up in some of its conceptual elements.

The concept 'idea' includes a certain *negative* moment. There is something which, in its nature, the idea does not achieve and does not provide, namely it does not give its object in complete adequacy, in a full and self-contained determination of its [14] essential elements. Individual characteristic moments of the object can, and certain definite ones must, be given in the idea.

The idea, one might say, gives its object only in a certain aphoristic illumination; depending on the nature of the available cognitive methodologies and other conditions of apprehension. Accidental characteristics may be conjectured, but the possibility always remains that new ones will emerge that attach themselves to, and modify, those already gained.

Although the idea does not provide the final indisputable determinateness of its object, it says and achieves essentially more than a fuzzy picture and presupposition. The emergence and attachment of new essential elements is not an empty formal-logical possibility, that is, a possibility which is accidental and arbitrary in respect of content. It is a determinate, essentially lawful possibility. Not its object, to be sure, but the idea itself is definitively determinable: in its meaning it leaves nothing open, it is a definitively determinable determinateness [*endgültig bestimmbare Bestimmtheit*]. This fulfillable, and, in the acquired idea, fulfilled determinateness, allows the necessarily unfulfillable determinateness (i.e. indeterminateness) of the idea's object to go over into a determinate indeterminateness. (Determinable determinateness of the idea – determinate indeterminateness of the idea's object.) The object always remains indeterminate, but this indeterminateness is itself determinate, determined in respect of the essential methodological possibilities and forms of an intrinsically unfulfillable determinability. The latter constitutes the essential structural content of the idea as such.

The determinable determinateness of the idea thus means: an unambiguously delimitable unitary contexture of meaning lawfully governed and motivated in its determinability by the never completely determined object. The [15] level of essential generality, and the kind of relevant motivations, depend upon the 'character of the content' (Paul Natorp: domain) of the idea's object, upon its regional essence.

b) The Circularity of the Idea of Primordial Science

Our problem is 'the idea of philosophy as primordial science'. How are we to obtain the essential determinative moments of this idea and thus the determinateness of the indeterminateness of the object? On which methodological path are they to be found? How is the determinable itself to be determined?

With this question, our problem is confronted by a difficulty of principle which must be squarely faced. The idea of philosophy as primordial science can and must, in so far as it is supposed to make visible precisely the origin and scope of the problem-*domain* of this science, itself be scientifically discovered and determined. It must itself be scientifically demonstrated, and, as primordially scientific, only by means of primordial-scientific method.

The idea of philosophy must in a certain way already be scientifically elaborated in order to define itself. But perhaps it is enough, in order to bring the object and its idea to determinateness, to become familiar with the main features of the method of primordial science. In any case the possibility exists, proceeding from elements of the genuine method, of pressing forward towards a new conception of the object.

At a higher level of the problematic we see the possibility of methodologically proceeding to the science in question (in a sense, directly). This possibility has its ultimate grounds in the meaning of all knowledge as such. Knowledge is itself an essential and original part of all method as such, and accordingly will prove itself in [16] an exemplary sense where there are the sharpest oppositions and most radical differences in the knowledge of objects, as well as in the objects of knowledge.

For this reason, once a genuine starting-point has been obtained for genuine philosophical method, the latter manifests its creative unveiling, so to speak, of new spheres of problems.

However, the sense of every genuine scientific method springs from the essence of the object of the science concerned, thus in our case the idea of philosophy. Primordial-scientific method cannot be derived from a nonprimordial, derivative science. Such an attempt must lead to blatant nonsense.

By their nature, ultimate origins can only be grasped from and in themselves. One must forthrightly deliver oneself over to the circle which lies within the very idea of primordial science. There is no escape from this, unless from the start one wants to avoid the difficulty and make the problem illusory through a cunning trick of reason (i.e. through a hidden absurdity).

The circularity of self-presupposition and self-grounding, of pulling oneself by one's own bootstraps out of the mire of natural life (the Münchhausen problem of the spirit), is not an artificial, cleverly constructed difficulty, but is already the expression of an essential characteristic of philosophy, and of the distinctive nature of its method. This method must put us in a position to *overcome* the apparently unavoidable circularity, in such a way that this circularity can be immediately seen as necessary and as belonging to the essence of philosophy.

While the above clarification of the nature of 'idea' is, according to strict methodological demands, still not fully adequate, it already presupposes insights that have their source in the idea to be defined, namely in the idea of primordial science itself. However, from the mere fact that we perceive the [17] circularity involved in defining the idea of philosophy, virtually nothing is achieved for the methodological prosecution of our investigation. Initially, we have no means of methodologically breaking out from this obstinate circularity. The search for the idea of philosophy presupposes that in some way we are already familiar with this idea as something capable of employment.

§ 3. The Way Out through the History of Philosophy

One way out suggests itself: everything spiritual has its genesis, its history. The particular sciences develop out of incomplete, methodologically unsure and awkward beginnings, to the height and purity of a genuine posing of problems and their solution. In the primitive stages, genuine insights are often already obtained, albeit mostly in bizarre guise. Also supporting this solution is the fact that contemporary philosophy is in essence historically oriented, not only in the sense that many philosophers pursue nothing but the history of philosophy, but especially in so far as either Kant or Aristotle provide the direction for philosophical research.

It is the intention of our problematic to show, in opposition to all previous philosophy, which takes worldview as a definite fundamental task or guiding intention, that worldview represents a phenomenon foreign to philosophy. However, this does mean that previous philosophy, in the course of its great and rich history, and irrespective of its close relation with the problem of worldview, did not come to genuinely philosophical knowledge, and even to the determination of authentic elements of its own nature. Our problematic – if it understands itself as arising from the essence of spirit – does not presume to condemn the whole history of philosophy as a gross error of the spirit, nor to radically exclude the possibility [18] that genuine elements towards the idea of philosophy as primordial science have been realized. Reflection on the history of philosophy will show that attempts to elevate philosophy to the rank of genuine science have not been rare.

It can be shown quite generally that in the course of its history philosophy has always stood in a definite connection to the idea of science; at one time, in the beginnings, it was simply identical with science; then it became, as πρώτη φιλοσοφία, the foundational science. In the essentially practical cultural age of Hellenism, enriched by life-possibilities flowing together from all lands, science in general, and as knowledge philosophy in particular, enters into the service of immediate life and becomes the art of the correct regulation of life. With the growing hegemony of the moral and especially the religious life-world, and with the exceptional spiritual power of emerging Christendom, science gets accorded the secondary position of a means, coming to typically pure expression in the medieval life-system. The period of high Scholasticism shows a powerful intensity of scientific consciousness, which, however, is at the same time dominated by the force and fullness of the genuinely inquiring religious life-world. The original motives and tendencies of the two life-worlds run into and converge in mysticism. The latter thereby takes on the character of the free flow of the life of consciousness. In this unchecked run-off of original motivations, the two life-worlds come into conflict. With Descartes there begins a radical self-reflection of knowledge; with Luther, the religious consciousness obtains a new position. Through the influence of the Greeks, the idea of science leads, via the Renaissance, to the epoch-making insights of Galileo, and the [19] mathematical science of nature is established. Philosophy itself demonstrates its propositions by geometric means, *more geometrico*. And once again knowledge pushes too far: there follows the critical deed of Kant, whose theory of knowledge claims to be not just science, but the scientific theory of theory. An analogous turning to philosophy as science occurs again in the nineteenth century, with the renewal of Kantianism in the Marburg school and in the school of value-philosophy.

But a clear consciousness of the problem of philosophy as science does not first occur in these late stages of the development of philosophy – stages themselves prepared through a rich history – but was already there in the first classical period of philosophy, in Plato's time. The attempt to constitute philosophy as genuine science thereby understood itself as a radical break from all previous philosophy: Μῦθόν τινα ἕκαστος φαίνεταί μοι διηγεῖσθαι παισὶν ὡς οὖσιν ἡμῖν – 'It seems to me that they [the old philosophers of being] told us stories, as if we were children.'[1] With this, Plato is thinking of the philosophers of nature, who assumed various kinds of being: the dry and the moist, the warm and the cold, love and hate. Such a philosophy had to express itself in scepticism and relativism, as in sophistry, whose leading doctrine states that man, indeed man in regard to his sensory perception, is the measure of all things. For this reason knowledge is impossible. There is only *opinion* (δόξα), which changes with time and circumstances. Such a shattering denial of every possibility of the valid grounding of truths, the deliverance of all knowledge over to arbitrariness and the mere contingency of opinion, aroused the sharpest opposition, which climaxed in the philosophical achievement of Socrates and above all of Plato. [20] Plato seeks τὴν ἀσφάλειαν τοῦ λόγου, the stable element of spirit; dialectic returns to the ultimate 'origins' of all presuppositions, of all propositions formulated in the sciences and also in the speech of everyday life: ἡ διαλεκτικὴ μέθοδος μόνη ταύτῃ πορεύεται, τὰς ὑποθέσεις ἀναιροῦσα, ἐπ᾽ αὐτὴν τὴν ἀρχὴν ἵνα βεβαιώσηται. Dialectic is the συμπεριαγωγὴ τέχνη τῆς ψυχῆς,[2] the scientific method of 'turning consciousness around', of setting forth the valid ideas which provide the ultimate grounding, foundation and original meaning of terms.

Already the crudest attempt to identify the main features of philosophy in its recognized significant epochs encounters a rich contexture of difficult fundamental problems. An unprejudiced immersion in Platonic philosophy must therefore somehow lead to the idea of philosophy, as indeed our 'way out through history' desires.

But are these truly philosophical problems? By what criterion is this particular epoch selected, and within this epoch Plato rather than the sophistry against which he fought? Appeal to common conviction, the *consensus omnium*, does not provide any scientific justification. Is philosophy genuine just through its historical factuality and through the fact of its name? What does historical factuality mean when it is not *comprehended*, that is, constituted in an historical consciousness? How should the comprehension of an historical philosophy be accomplished? For example, the concept of ἀνάμνησις in Platonic philosophy: does this simply mean recollection, comprehended in the context of Plato's doctrine of the immortality of the soul? A sensualist psychology will dismiss this as mythology. Experimental psychology will make quite other claims concerning the explanation of [21] memory; perhaps it will reject the Platonic considerations on this subject as crude, scientifically useless beginnings, the results of naive, pre-scientific reflection. Yet genuine philosophy as primordial science finds that with this concept and its intended essence Plato saw deeply into the problematic of pure consciousness. Which conception is the true one? What is the genuine fact [*Tatsache*]? Clearly, a comprehension of Platonic philosophy that is guided by the idea of genuine philosophy will draw out something of philosophical benefit from history. But of course, in this case the idea of philosophy and at least a portion of its genuine realization is already presupposed. Genuine philosophical insights which present themselves in primitive formulas can be recognized as such only with the help of a standard, a criterion of genuineness.

There is no genuine history of philosophy at all without an historical consciousness which itself lives in genuine philosophy. Every history and history of philosophy *constitutes* itself in life in and for itself, life which is itself *historical* in an absolute sense. Admittedly, all this runs very much counter to the attitude of the 'experience'-proud historians of facts who consider that only they themselves are scientific, and who believe that facts can be found like stones on a path! Therefore the way out through the history of philosophy, as a way of arriving at essential elements of the philosophical idea, is hardly desirable from a *methodological and scientific* point of view. It is illusory because, strictly speaking, without the idea of philosophy as primordial science what belongs in the history of philosophy and what in other historical contexts cannot even be circumscribed.

§ 4. The Way Out through the Philosopher's Scientific Attitude of Mind [22]

Our problem is the idea of philosophy as primordial science; *more precisely*, it is *first* the discovery of a methodological way that can provide secure access to the essential elements of the idea of philosophy as primordial science.

One might think that the attempt to arrive at the idea of philosophy from history must necessarily fail, because the rich diversity of systems, and of theories that in part contradict one another, cannot be brought under a common concept. Since the variety of content makes a criterion of selection necessary, an *induction* based on comparative considerations is impossible. However, if one does not hold fast to the systems, namely to the substantive doctrinal content of the individual philosophies, but turns back to the essential character of their creators, i.e. to the typically philosophical form of thought, then beyond the diversity of content the unity of philosophical attitude will emerge. Inquiry is not thereby directed to historical and human individuality, the personality of the philosopher, but to the latter as expressing a particular type of spirituality, the philosophical type. In the present day, Simmel has made this attempt by inverting the characterization of art: it has been said that art is a world-picture seen through a personal temperament; by contrast, Simmel claims that philosophy is a temperament seen through a world-picture, that is, philosophy is the expression of a typical stance and experiential form of spirit. As a result of this interpretation of philosophy, a significant philosophical achievement cannot be measured according to the scientific concept of truth, that is, by asking how far its doctrine corresponds with the object, with Being. [23] It has its original value as a primordial, objective formation of a typical human consciousness. The 'truth' of a philosophy is therefore independent of the substantive content of its propositions.

Apart from the fact that, in this case also, the same methodological difficulties arise concerning the criterion of selection for personalities who are to count as philosophers, this attempt to establish the idea of philosophy from the typical spirituality of the philosopher, from the spiritual type of philosophy's genuine custodians, falls outside the framework of our problematic. It is easy to see that the concept of philosophy here coincides with that of the creator of an original worldview. If initially no argument for this can be advanced, and the presumption arises that the scientific philosopher might also be intended, it must in any case be said, concerning the indicated unscientific concept of truth, that this doubtless has a meaning in specific spheres of life, but not in connection with the idea of philosophy as *primordial science*. The idea of philosophy as primordial science cannot be worked out from the idea of a scientific stance of the spirit. This is not to deny that philosophy as primordial science corresponds to a typical and special life-relation, indeed in a quite definite sense as the subjective correlate of a typical spiritual constitution. But this phenomenon can meaningfully be studied only on the basis of the constitution of the *idea* of philosophy, and from the living fulfilment of the motivations exacted by it.

§ 5. The Way Out through Inductive Metaphysics

Once again we put the question: *how* are we to arrive at the essential elements for a full determination of the idea of philosophy as primordial science? [24] *As* primordial science: what is thereby given is an essential but hitherto unconsidered clue as to the domain in which philosophy belongs.

In this way, the possibilities for defining the idea are already essentially restricted, and not only through a preliminary negative demarcation. Philosophy is neither art (poetry) nor world-wisdom (the provision of practical rules). The possible direction for defining the idea is already positively prefigured. Philosophy is – more precisely, should be – still more precisely: it is a problem as science, and indeed as primordial science. But we immediately recall the circularity in the concept of primordial science, more particularly in the latter's grounding. In whatever way one initially takes the concept, it means something ultimate or, better, original, primordial, not in a temporal sense but substantively, first in relation to primary grounding and constitution: *principium*. In comparison with primordial science, every particular scientific discipline is not *principium* but *principatum*, the derivative and not the originary, the sprung-from [*Ent-sprungene*] and not the primal spring [*Ur-sprung*], the origin.

It is meaningful to deduce the derivative from the origin; the reverse is nonsense. However, precisely from the derivative I can go back to the origin as spring (since the river flows, I can return to its source). Although it is absurd, and precisely because it is absurd, to wish to derive primordial science from any particular science (or the totality thereof), the possibility of a *methodological return* to primordial science from the particular sciences is necessary and illuminating. Further: every particular science is as such derivative. It is therefore evident that, from *each and every* particular science (whether actual or merely possible), there is a *way* leading back to its origin, to primordial science, to philosophy.

If, therefore, we are to solve the problem as to how our own problematic – the concretion of the idea of philosophy *as* primordial science – can be scientifically validated, [25] this must be through a methodological return from the non-original to the origin. In other words, the particular sciences form the methodological starting-point for the solution to our problem, the sphere in which we locate ourselves. Where in these disciplines is the motive for the return to primordial science?

Let us place ourselves within a specific science: physics, for example. It works with rigorous methods and proceeds with the sureness of genuine science. It seeks to apprehend the being of lifeless nature in its lawfulness, in particular the lawfulness of its *movements*. Movement, whether conceived in mechanical, thermodynamic, or electrodynamic terms, is the basic phenomenon. *Every one of its propositions rests on experience, on factual knowledge*; and each of its theories, even the most general, is a theory within and for physical experience, is supported or 'refuted' by such experience.

From this particular science we wish to proceed to primordial science. What characterizes physics as a particular science, what is *particular* to it? What is there about it, therefore, which cannot be accommodated in the idea of primordial science? Clearly, every science is knowledge, and as such is knowledge of an object. The object of physics is the world of bodies, material nature. Excluded from this domain of objects is 'living' nature, the sphere of the biological sciences. The object is not the totality but a part or particular sector thereof. But natural science as a whole, all the particular natural sciences taken together, is also a particular science. It does not include the human spirit, with its achievements and works as they have developed in history and been objectified in culture, and which themselves constitute their own specific object-domain, that of the sciences of the spirit.

But nature and spirit do not exhaust the possible object-domains of the sciences. We think of mathematics, for example, as geometry and [26] as analysis. In contrast to the previously mentioned *'concrete'* sciences, we call these *'abstract'* sciences. But they are also particular sciences: geometry treats the specific phenomenon of space, as well as ideal space, the theory of elliptical functions – or algebraic analysis (the doctrine of irrational and imaginary numbers). Although all these disciplines are certainly 'abstract', they have specific object-domains in which the methodology of their knowledge operates. Theology also, which as the doctrine of God as the Absolute could be called primordial science, is a particular science. That is evident from the role that the historical, which belongs to the essence of Christianity, plays within this science. I mention in passing that in neither Protestant nor Catholic theology has a methodologically clear concept of this science so far been achieved; indeed, apart from some incomplete attempts in recent Protestant theology, there is not the slightest awareness that there is a profound problem here, a problem, however, which can only be rigorously taken up in the sphere of a problematic still to be developed.

The field of objects of any science presents itself as a particular sector; every such field has its boundary at another, and no science can be found which encompasses all fields. The ground of the individuation of the sciences is the boundedness of their object-domains. It must, therefore, also be here that the motive lies for returning from the particular science to primordial science. The latter will not be a science of separate object-domains, but of what is common to them all, the science not of a particular, but of universal being. But this can only be arrived at from the individual sciences through induction. Its determination is dependent on the final results of the particular sciences, to the extent that these are at all oriented to the general. [27] In other words, this science would have no cognitive function whatever to call its own; it would be nothing else than a more or less uncertain, hypothetical repetition and overview of what the particular sciences, through the exactness of their methods, have already established. Above all, since this science would be result rather than origin, and would itself be founded through the individual sciences, it would not in the slightest degree correspond to the idea of primordial science. Even the problematic of the ultimate primal cause of being, although seemingly autonomous and novel *vis-à-vis* the particular sciences, would make no difference, for the methodological character of this reversed problem is still natural-scientific. (Demonstration of the historical connections between Aristotle's metaphysics of nature and that of the middle ages.)

I have not invented the concept of such a science in a constructive-dialectical fashion. Under the name of *inductive metaphysics*, it is regarded as a possible science by influential philosophical currents of the present day, and correspondingly prosecuted. This philosophical tendency, which also expresses itself epistemologically in critical realism (Külpe, Messer, Driesch), has recently been enthusiastically received in the theology of both confessions. This is a further demonstration of the radical mis-recognition of the authentic problems of theology, the science which, because it has expected from the sciences of nature and history something (if it understood itself correctly) it had no right to expect, has more than any other fallen victim to the groundless naturalism and historicism of the nineteenth century.

What has been said concerning inductive metaphysics is not meant to be an adequate critique, but only to show that, in a purely formal sense, an inductive metaphysics is in no way adequate to the idea of an absolute primordial science.

Consequently, the mode of return from the particular sciences, the motive we have followed in starting out from these latter, [28] is unten-able. Sciences are unities, contexts of knowledge with content. We characterize them as particular in respect of their objects of knowledge. Is there any other way of looking at the matter? Clearly there is. Instead of the object of knowledge, we can focus on the knowledge of the object. With knowledge, we come to a phenomenon which must truly apply to all sciences, which indeed makes every science what it is.

CHAPTER TWO

Critique of Teleological-Critical Method [29]

§ 6. Knowledge and Psychology

Knowing is a psychic process. As such it is bound by the lawfulness of psychic life and is itself the object of the science of the psychic: psychology. Psychic facts, whether conceived in a natural-scientific manner or normatively through other laws, are at any rate facts. The psychic contexture of life is scientifically accessible only in psychological experience. Although knowledge is indeed a necessary phenomenon in all sciences, considered as something psychic it constitutes a restricted region of objects. Physical nature, and even less the mathematical, cannot be traced back to the psychic or derived from it. Psychology too is a special science, the distinctive *special science of the spirit*. It is not, like some other special sciences, e.g. mathematics, an ideal science, i.e. independent of experience and thus possessing absolute validity. Such ideal sciences, considered as works of the spirit, are at the same time possible objects of the empirical science of spirit, of (higher) psychology. The latter, were it to be the primordial science we are seeking, would have to make possible the 'derivation' of the absolute validity of mathematical knowledge.

It is absurd, however, to want to ground absolute knowledge on a special empirical science which itself does not rest on absolutely valid knowledge. The initial [30] difficulty was from *where* the idea is to be reached. This *where*, this sphere, appears to be found, but at the same time the *how* is problematic.

The complete traversal of all the particular sciences as science led to a genuine common feature: their character as knowledge. This, however, is a phenomenon which does not itself belong in such a domain of objects, which is of such generality and substantive incipience that from it all possible knowledge could experience its *ultimate* grounding. Knowledge, however, is a phenomenon of a quite specific region of being, the psychic.

But as Kant already saw, there is an ambiguity in the concept of the psychic. Psychology as empirical science, as essentially natural-scientific experience, certainly seeks laws governing the psychic processes of representations and their association. But what is peculiar is that the psychic also manifests a quite different kind of lawfulness: every science works with definite universal concepts and principles through which the immediately given is ordered. The 'incalculable multiplicity' of the empirical becomes, through conceptual restriction, comprehensible, and, through a single leading viewpoint, homogeneous. Thus, according to Rickert, all the natural sciences – amongst which he counts psychology – are *generalizing*; they consider empirical reality in respect of its ultimate and most universal characteristics (laws of motion). The cultural sciences, by contrast, are *individualizing*; they consider empirical reality in its individuality, peculiarity and uniqueness. And these are known through their relation to a (cultural) value which itself has the character of universality.

§ 7. The Axiomatic Fundamental Problem [31]

Underlying all knowledge therefore – the inductive as also the deductive sciences, and irrespective of specific scientific and methodological theories – there are ultimate concepts, basic principles and axioms. Only through these axioms can anything be established about facts and from facts. Through such axioms, as normative laws, sciences first become sciences. Axioms are the origin or 'primal leap' [*Ur-sprung*] of knowledge, and the science which has these origins for its own object is primordial science, philosophy. '*The problem of philosophy is [therefore] the validity of the axioms.*'[1] Here I take account only of theoretical (logical) axioms, simply for illustration; for the moment ethical and aesthetic axioms will be left aside.

Axioms are norms, laws, principles, i.e. 'representational connections'. Their validity is to be demonstrated. Here the difficulty inherent in the idea of primordial science once again shows itself: *how are axioms to be proven?* They cannot be deductively arrived at through other still more universal principles, for they are themselves the *first* (fundamental) principles from which every other principle is demonstrable. Just as little can axioms be indirectly derived from facts, for they are already presupposed for the conception of a fact as fact (its subordination under universal concepts), as also for the methodological process of induction.

That we are once again confronted by this frequently mentioned difficulty, characteristic of the task of grounding the origin and inception, is a sign that we are operating in the sphere of primordial science. Indeed, [32] apparently without noticing it, and after various unsuccessful attempts, we have arrived at the primordial science from the individual sciences. The mediation was achieved by psychology; it must therefore occupy the critical position. The undeniably common character of all knowledge as psychic process led back to a particular science, psychology, but to psychology as an empirical and particular science, which can be conceived as a natural science of the psychic analogous to the physical sciences.

The step towards a new 'lawfulness in the psychical' already brought us into the realm of primordial science, i.e. to its distinctive feature (the circularity of grounding). Therefore this *other* lawfulness 'in the psychical' is a sign of a genuine primordial-scientific, i.e. philosophical, problem.

Of course, the concepts of 'the psychic', of 'law', and of 'norm', remain completely unexplained. The unrefined state of the conceptual materials employed means that it is initially inexplicable how the psychic should be governed by a double lawfulness, one natural-scientific and the other something different; nor is it explicable how the psychic governed by natural law should be accessible through an additional normativity.

In conjunction with the introduction of a new lawfulness in the psychical, knowledge as a psychical phenomenon also comes under a new lawfulness that would apprehend it. Knowledge is now considered as *true* in so far as it possesses validity. The normative consideration of knowledge separates out a preferred class: true knowledge is distinguished by its particular value. This value is intelligible only because true knowledge in itself has the character of value. Truth in itself is validity and as such something valuable.

'Philosophy concerns itself with the validity of those representational connections which, themselves unprovable, ground all proof with immediate evidence.'[2] *How [33] is the immediate evidence of axioms to be shown?* How, i.e. in what way, by what method?

To be sure, posing the problem in this form is still vague, but in comparison with our initial and very general attempts it already has a more concrete form. At least one thing has become evident, namely that this problematic, which is connected with the ultimate principles and axioms presupposed by any particular science, is utterly distinctive, and as such can never be the object of a particular science. The particular sciences are divided according to the diversity and specificity of their *knowledge*. Philosophy has their unity for its object, their unitary sense *as knowledge*. The particular sciences may become ever more perfected and may extend to previously unknown new domains, their boundaries may become fluid as they all strive for the idea of a unitary science; they nevertheless presuppose the meaning of knowledge in general and the question of the validity of the axioms which they themselves apply.

How is philosophy to demonstrate this validity? How, i.e. by what method? *What is the appropriate method for grounding the validity of axioms?* The axioms are supposed to be a new kind of law in the psychic. First of all, therefore, the nature of the psychic and its possible lawfulness must be described.

§ 8. Teleological-Critical Method of Finding Norms

The psychic is a complex of temporally flowing experiential processes which build upon each other and proceed from one another according to definite general laws. Every psychic fact is governed by general rules of coexistence and succession. The movement of spiritual life subject to natural laws is governed by causal necessity. Among other things, psychology [34] investigates the way we actually think, putting forward laws concerning thought as thought, as a specific kind of psychic process. Now alongside this lawfulness of compulsion, of 'the must', there is another kind of 'ideal determination', that of 'the ought'. Over against psychical necessity stands a command. This normative law tells us how facts, therefore thought, ought to be, in order that thought be universally sanctioned as true and valid.

What meaning does it have to place the psychic functions of human beings under two different kinds of lawfulness? The 'same life of the soul' is object of an explanatory science, and then also object of 'ideal assessments'[3] – themselves ultimately a norm, albeit of a methodological rather than a constitutive type. A law of nature is a principle of explanation, a norm is a principle of evaluation [*Beurteilung*]. The two kinds of lawfulness are not identical, but they are also not absolutely different from each other.

The natural laws of the psychic do not include normative laws or decide anything about them. But they also do not exclude the fulfilment of a norm. 'Among the vast number of representational connections there are only a few that possess the value of normativity.'[4] The logical norms are *definite types of representational connection* alongside others, distinguished only by the value of normativity. 'A norm is a particular form of psychic movement governed by the natural laws of psychological life.'[5] The system of norms presents a selection from the manifold of possible representational associations. What principle does the selection follow? 'Logical normativity [35] is demanded by representational activity only in so far as this activity ought to fulfil the goal of being true.'[6]

Just as natural laws of psychic thought-processes contain assertions about how we in fact – according to natural law – necessarily think, so do norms tell us how we *ought to* think, provided only that truth is the goal of our thought.

The character of normative laws and normative validities must be discovered and grounded by a method that differs from that of natural science. Their nature and validation are determined by truth as the goal of thinking. In view of this aim – universal validity – they are selected according to pre-established requirements. Norms are necessary in regard to the *telos* of *truth*.

They can be sorted out and selected in their focus on this goal. The appropriate method for identifying and grounding norms is the *teleological* method or, as it is otherwise called, the *critical method*. This method is totally different from the methods of the particular sciences, which are all oriented towards establishing and explaining facts. It grounds a quite new fundamental type of science. With this method philosophy begins; in our case, since we have been initially concerned with processes of knowledge, logic begins as distinct from psychology: 'Presupposing that there are perceptions, representations, and combinations of these according to laws of psychological mechanism, logic itself begins with the conviction that matters cannot rest there, and that in the sphere of representational connections, however these may arise, a distinction can be made between truth and untruth, that in the last instance there are forms [36] to which these connections correspond and laws which they *should* obey.'[7]

But does this teleological method, different as it is from the genetic method (of psychology), in principle go beyond factual science, i.e. can it establish anything over and above the factic and the factically valid; does it achieve what is demanded of it? The attempt to reflect on 'normal' consciousness will discover nothing except the *factually existing* forms and norms of psychic thought-processes in individual consciousness, forms and norms which guide and govern all judgement, conceptualization and inference. These may be immediately evident for my individual consciousness – but this immediate evidence is often very deceptive and thus inadequate as a criterion for the philosophical grounding of axioms, which grounding, as primordial-scientific, is supposed to transcend individual and historically conditioned opinion.

The proof of the a priori validity of axioms cannot itself be carried out in an empirical way. How then is philosophical method able to exclude everything individual, conditioned, historical and accidental? How can this unclouded axiomatic consciousness, which grounds the validity of axioms, be achieved? Is philosophical method really so constituted that it can ground the supra-individual?

Does the teleological method, according to its basic tendency, go in this direction? In fact it does, for it inquires not into what *hic et nunc* is factically recognized as thought-form and norm, but into *those* norms which, corresponding to the goal of universally valid thought, *should* be recognized. The universality and necessity of the *should* is not *factical* and empirical, but *ideal* and absolute.

[37] Fichte, in continuing Kant's critical thought, was the first to recognize teleology as the method of the doctrine of science [*Wissenschaftslehre*], i.e. as the method of philosophy. For the first time, Fichte sought to derive systematically the forms of intuition and thought, the axioms and fundamental principles of the understanding, and the ideas of reason (all of which Kant, in the metaphysical and transcendental deduction, attempted to establish as the conditions of the possibility of the knowing consciousness) from a unitary principle and according to rigorous method, as the system of necessary actions of reason demanded by the very goal of reason. Reason can and must be understood only from itself; its laws and norms cannot be derived from a context external to it. The ego is egological deed-action [*Tathandlung*], it has to be active, its goal is the ought [*das Sollen*]. In acting it sets itself a limit, but only in order to be able to lift [*aufheben*] it again. The ought is the ground of Being.

Fichte did indeed work out the teleological idea in a radical manner, seeking the goal of reason in itself, as it gives itself in absolute self-knowing and self-insight. But he was also convinced that from this simple primordial act [*Urakt*] of the ego the multiplicity and diversity of qualitatively different functions of reason could be derived through pure deduction, i.e. through a constant and repeated overcoming of the posited limit. His teleological method was transformed into a constructive dialectic. What Fichte overlooked was that the teleological method requires a substantive material guideline in which the goal of reason might realize itself, and in which the actions of reason are themselves to be discovered in their universal character. This material, the empirical psychic context, does provide the determinations of content for thought-forms and norms, but it does not *ground* their validity. It is, so to speak, only an occasion and impetus for finding them – they are *grounded* in a teleological manner.

[38] The modern teleological-critical method grounds and demonstrates the validity of axioms by setting them out as necessary means to the ideal goal of universally valid truth, and always 'by reference to experience'. Reflection upon the 'correct' teleologically necessary *Gestalt* of the forms and norms of reason must always connect with characteristics of the thought-process as revealed (albeit in the roughest way) by psychology. However, the normative validity of axioms cannot be grounded by psychic *facts as facts*. Psychology as an empirical science *never provides grounds for axiomatic validity*. The latter is grounded in the *'teleological meaning'* of the axioms themselves, 'which employs them as means for the goal of universal validity'.

Psychology as empirical science is not a philosophical discipline. What philosophy takes from it is only material, which it handles by a brand-new teleological methodology. For example, philosophy takes from psychology the meaning of the psychical functions of thinking, willing and feeling, from which clue it seeks out the three normative regions of the true, the good and the beautiful. Were this psychological division to be overturned, 'so perhaps would the division of philosophy collapse along with it, not however the certainty of norms and axioms, which do not rest upon these empirical-psychological concepts, but have just come to consciousness with their assistance'.[8]

In the last resort psychology offers only formal characteristics; formations of the content of rational values are first shown in history, which is the authentic *organon* of critical philosophy. The historical formations of cultural life are the real empirical occasion for critical-teleological reflection. Not only does history reveal a multiplicity of formations, [39] but in this way it guards against relativism. (Absolute validity not in itself a time-value?!) *The constant change of these formations in the historical process* preserves philosophy from historicism, from stopping with particular historically determined formations and dispensing with the apprehension of absolute validity. The latter is the ineluctable aim of philosophy, and the method proper to it is the teleological, i.e. reflection upon the ideal ought as the principle of critical valuational judgement for everything that is.

§ 9. The Methodological Function of Material Pregivenness

Our intention is to press methodically into the realm of primordial science and thus to arrive at essential elements of the idea of philosophy. The path leads from the particular sciences to the task of exposing the ultimate forms and norms of thought. Such exposition means determination according to content and the grounding of validity. This *fundamental axiomatic problem* shows the index of primordial science (circularity). In our context this is a sign of a genuine problematic.

The fundamental axiomatic problem is essentially a problem of method. The critical-teleological method, in accordance with its novel aim of establishing not factualities or statements of experience as such, but what is prior to all experiences as their conditions of possibility, as a necessary *ought to*-be in its ideal validity, emerged as a new kind of method in contrast to the modes of grounding in any particular science.

How then do we decide whether the critical-teleological method succeeds or fails in what is required of it? The only obvious possibility is that [40] the critical-teleological method *demonstrates from itself* its primordial-scientific suitability or unsuitability through an analysis of its own structure. Other criteria are not permissible for a primordial-scientific phenomenon.

The structural analysis of the critical-teleological method must first take account of the *essential transformation* – more precisely, the *ultimate motive* thereof – that method has undergone in contemporary transcendental philosophy as compared with the form it assumed in Fichte's system of absolute idealism.

This transformation is due to insight into the inner impossibility of a *dialectical*-teleological deduction of the system of necessary actions and necessary forms of reason. Dialectic in the sense of resolving ever newly posited contradictions is *substantively uncreative*; moreover the positing of contradictions is itself possible only through a hidden non-dialectical principle which on account of its own hiddenness and unclarity is not in a position to ground the character and validation of the deduced forms and norms as genuine ones. The dialectic of antithesis and synthesis cannot be activated by itself: it remains condemned to an unproductive standstill, or else it unfolds itself on the implicit and methodologically arbitrary basis of something substantively given, or at least presupposed.

The transformation aims therefore – more according to instinct, more under the influence of the nineteenth-century ideal of science than from a clearly developed insight into the inner impossibility of constructive dialectic – to avoid the *way-out speculation* of every kind of deductive dialectic. The teleological method receives a solid foundation in the objective domains of psychology and history. To be sure, alongside this 'transcendental empiricism', the important philosophical school of the 'Marburgers' proceeds in a new direction, towards a dialectic which brings them into close proximity to Hegel.

[41] Empirical-scientific results are in a definite sense necessary pre-suppositions of the teleological method. With respect to what is given in experience, in relation to factually given psychic processes, I can now pose the question of *which of them* are necessary to the goal of thought. Which particular forms and norms of thought fulfil the ideal goal, or are necessary means for the ideal fulfilment of this goal?

This selection, therefore, which stands under the criterion of the ideal aim of universally valid (true) thought, presupposes the *givenness of that which can be selected* and teleologically *evaluated*. Teleological-axiomatic grounding would lose all sense *without a pregiven* chooseable and assessable *something*, a *what*.

Psychology and history remove the basic deficiency of dialectical method through their *methodological function of providing already given material*.

The consideration of the way in which *dialectical*-teleological method is transformed into *critical*-teleological method already yielded an *element of the latter's authentic structure*: the provision of a material basis. The authentic function of critical selection, evaluation and grounding of axioms, is built upon this foundation-laying element of method.

The question of structural analysis now becomes *decisive*: what is the meaning of this way of construction, and how does this founding context look? *Why decisive?* Teleological method is supposed to serve the primordial-scientific purpose of grounding the axiomatic element.

When empirical elements come into play, elements that are not primordial-scientific, does not this involve a fundamental *deformation of method* from the very beginning? Everything depends on whether the preliminary function of empirically giving material leaves the teleological evaluation as such untouched and uncontaminated. Does this function extend beyond its proper sense of providing material for evaluative [42] judgement? Apparently not. The material is simply given. Teleological value-judgement is built independently upon material which is taken simply as its support. 'Therefore' (what psychology provides) will according to Lotze not itself be pertinent: psychology has nothing more to do; it provides the pregiven material, and then, as it were, withdraws, its role exhausted. New criteria and new kinds of procedure come into play. Let us assume, therefore, that psychological results concerning processes of thought are available.

§ 10. Giving of Ideals as the Core Element of Method. Misunderstanding of the Problematic of Primordial Science

The decisive question now arises: what are the necessary forms and norms that bring thought to universal validity and thus fulfil the goal of truth? This is the teleological method reduced to its simplest form. Let us see what belongs to the sense of this method.

Thought has to be true; thought that is not true must be considered as ungenuine, worthless thought. The goal is desired because it is obligatory. This obligatoriness [*Sollen*] itself presupposes a valuational orientation. What is held to be valuable? Truth.

Teleologically requisite, necessary determinations of thought are such as to form thought according to its ideal. The goal is universal validity of thought, its truth.

In carrying out the critical-teleological method, I have before me the pregiven material, the universal characteristics, for example, of psychic thought-processes. Having this present, at the same time I direct my attention to the ideal of thought. With this in view, I determine from the given material [43] those elements that are necessary conditions for the realization of the ideal.

The focus of the whole method lies in the ideal of thought; more precisely, in visualizing the provision of the ideal. The possibility of carrying through the method depends on the norm-giving ideal itself. Leaving aside for the moment, without further structural analysis, the act of value-judgement wherein the given material is put in normative relation to the ideal, let us look at the goal-consciousness that first makes this act possible.

Teleological method includes within itself consciousness of the ideal, of a definite relation to the goal as such. *Or* does the simple conviction of the value of truth suffice: do I want the truth, and in this wanting reflect upon the rules to which my thought should conform, upon the forms it should follow in order that it will correspond to my aim? Experience clearly shows that, in order to fulfil the demands of true thinking, I do not always need an explicit consciousness of the ideal of thought. Thousands of people think factually and correctly without any consciousness of this ideal.

However, teleological method is more than a way of actually thinking and thinking truly. It seeks to be the methodological means to raise explicitly to consciousness the norms and forms, in themselves and as such, to which natural thinking conforms. It seeks to know thinking and knowledge themselves. *The clear consciousness of the ideal of thought is therefore necessary*. Providing the ideal first makes possible a judgemental and selective relation to the material. How do I bring to consciousness the ideal of thought, i.e. the goal towards which all genuine thought ought to strive? The goal of thought is 'universal validity'. What do validity and universal validity mean? What thinking is universally valid? *True* thinking. What does truth mean? What are [44] the constitutive moments that make truth what it is, the moments that determine *the* goal thought ought to realize? These questions concerning the constitutive and defining elements of truth, of the ideal, i.e. the criterion of value-judgement in teleological method, are in fact the same questions which are to be decided with the assistance of teleological method.

The structural analysis of the critical-teleological method shows that this method presupposes, in its most proper sense and as the condition of its own possibility, just what it is supposed to arrive at. It cannot by itself find its own foundation, because in order to carry out its task in the methodologically prescribed way the ideal must already be given as the criterion of critical normative evaluation. Supposing, however, that the ideal, the standard of oughtness, were 'somehow' found, then the problem for whose sake it was discovered would already be solved and the method would be illusory. *If the method in its purported sense is to be possible, then it is also already superfluous,* and criticism could at this point break off.

It has already become clear, purely from the analysis of its meaning, that the method undermines itself. It rests 'somehow' on a misunderstanding of the genuine problematic of primordial science. But we have not yet examined the matter with sufficient precision. The analysis remained at a penultimate stage. We saw that the fulfilment, more accurately the very approach of the method, includes the *having-present of the ideal*, the goal, the ought. The ideal manifestly has a content, it has substantive determinations. It is, however, an ideal, not a factual content but an ought relation. This ought character stands over against every Being as the moment of ideality and supra-empirical validity. Therefore, in the meaning of teleological method, something essentially more and essentially different is presupposed: the *givenness of the ought*, such that the absolute ought becomes *primordial objectivity*. [45] How does an ought give itself at all, what is its subject-correlate? A Being [*Sein*] becomes theoretically known, but an ought? So long as the original experiential directedness of the lived experience [*Erlebnis*] of the ought, of ought-giving and ought-taking, is not set forth, the already problematical method remains obscure at its very core. The inclusion of the ought-phenomenon within teleological method means that the latter can no longer be seen as a pure theoretical structure. This of course does not say anything against its suitability for primordial-scientific purposes, especially since the critical-transcendental philosophy of Rickert already sees theory as value-laden and necessarily ought-related.[9] Where without the slightest discomforture – since one is absolutely blind to the whole world of problems implied in the phenomenon of the ought – the concept of the ought finds philosophical employment, there we find unscientific idle talk, which is not ennobled by the fact that this ought is made into the foundation stone of an entire system. On the other hand, this fixation on the ought is a sign that the philosophical problematic has been entered into more deeply than usual. Although the phenomenon and its position of primacy remain unclarified, genuine motives are certainly involved, and one needs only to follow up on them.

However, let us inquire further into the immanent character of the sense of method. Supposing the method were clarified to the extent of showing that, in connection with the preliminary function of bare theoretical (?) material givenness (of psychic thought-processes in the crudest form), there is a new kind of lived experience of the ought, of the giving of ideals. Does a blind power announce itself in the ought-experience ('thrust into conscience'), or does this ought give itself as self-certifying? If the latter, on what basis self-certifying? Why should a thought-process correspond to the ideal? Because otherwise it would be an incorrect, ungenuine thought, of a sort [46] that would have no value. Because, therefore, the ideal is valuable, and in itself presents a value, it ought to be realized through my thinking. I experience it, I 'live' it as an ought. Does a value announce itself in the specific kind of experience that relates to the ought, a value that grounds the ideal in its absolute intrinsic validity, so that in the experience of the ought a value is constituted? 'Whoever strives after truth subordinates himself to an ought, just like the person who fulfils his duty.'[10]

But is every value given to me as an ought? Clearly not. I experience value-relations without the slightest element of ought being given. In the morning I enter the study; the sun lies over the books, etc., and I delight in this. Such delight is in no way an ought; 'delightfulness' as such is not given to me in an ought-experience. I ought to work, I ought to take a walk: two motivations, two possible kinds of 'because' which do not reside in the delightful itself but presuppose it. There is, therefore, a kind of lived experience in which I take delight, in which the valuable as such is given.

If the ideal, the goal of knowledge, truth, is a value, this does not at all need to announce itself in an ought. The value is something in and for itself, not an ought, but just as little a Being [*ein Sein*]. The value 'is' not, but rather it 'values' in an intransitive sense: in being worth-taking [*Wertnehmen*], 'it values' for me, for the value-experiencing subject. 'Valuing' becomes an object only through formalization. 'Object' is a misleading designation: our language is not adequate to the new basic type of lived experience involved here.

The sense of the teleological method undoubtedly implies the moment of the ought-experience. If, as the interpretation has shown, the ideal is a value, then this must constitute itself in the original manner of value-giving upon which the ought is founded. But this is not to say that every ought must be founded in a value; a Being [*ein Sein*] can also found an ought. Another novel structure of original [47] constitution occurs when I say: 'Something has meaning.' Phenomenon of 'realization of meaning' in the narrower sense; both substantively complex.

With every step of the analysis, the method is shown to be fraught with presuppositions. The method wants to be primordial science, assuming phenomena that are initially problematic but that still pose for us the important problem of whether – and how – they are possible as component parts of primordial-scientific theoretical methodology. In this way the teleological method, precisely in its core element of the giving of ideals, has emerged as even more highly complicated.

§ 11. Investigation of the Claim to Primordial Science by the Teleological-Critical Method

a) Truth and Value

Until now we have inquired into the meaning of teleological method itself, as it presents itself, but in a manner whereby connections and new kinds of phenomena, which the method's advocates do not see at all, have already become visible to us.

The further question, for which we are now to some degree prepared, of whether the teleological method makes a *rightful* claim for itself, will carry the critique further.

What is its principled claim? As long as we stand on the ground of the method itself and go along with it, we can expose new phenomena and clarify the method to itself. *If* the ideal (truth) is a value, then the method must also be originally constituted in a value-giving.

But *is* truth in any way a value? One will hardly dare to dispute that. Truth is characterized *as* a value [48], and it is explained *as* a value in terms of specific contextures. (From this point on, the train of thought for the problem is to be essentially reversed.)

Essence [*Wesen*] can also found the ought. These primitive elements of a genuine philosophical problematic require more comprehensive investigation. One thing is evident, namely that Rickert saw an important phenomenon when he identified the object of knowledge as the ought and marked it off from the psychic mechanism: the phenomenon of motivation, which has its primary meaning in the problem of knowledge as well as in other problems.

It is one thing to *declare something as a value*, another to *take something as a value in a 'worth-taking'*. The latter can be characterized as an originary phenomenon of origin, a constituting of life in and for itself. The former must be seen as derivative, as founded in the theoretical, and as itself a theoretical phenomenon dependent on lived life in itself. It presupposes the theoretical highlighting of the character of value as such. The more precise stratification of this phenomenon does not interest us here.

The question arises as to whether truth as such constitutes itself in an original worth-taking. Of course not, one will say, because truth is 'abstract', and only something concrete can be experienced as valuable. Let us admit this, and look at examples of true knowledge, e.g. true propositions such as '2 times 2 equals 4' or 'Napoleon I died on the island of St Helena'. Some of you are sufficiently advanced methodologically to isolate these examples: no valuing as such occurs in these propositions. One will hardly fall victim to a natural confusion; I have chosen these two true propositions intentionally. One could think: numbers are 'values' and multiplication itself yields a 'value'. Quantities as 'values' are a separate problem, which our question does not touch. It is a matter not of the content of a judgement, but of its truth. Is being-true itself given as a value? By no means, also not [49] in the second case of an historical judgement. To be sure, the substantive content of this judgement involves something value-like in the sense of 'historically significant'. But this phenomenon, although it plays a methodological role in the constitution of historical truth, does not touch upon being-true as such. Being-true (ἀ-λήθεια) does not as such 'value'. I experience worth-taking in the delightful as delightful, I simply live in the truth as truth. I do not apprehend being-true in and through a worth-taking. A possible objection is that this might apply in the indicated cases, namely that precisely *I*, who am standing here, do not have, or someone else does not have, a 'value-tinged' experience. Other people will experience the propositions differently. At any rate, the question cannot always be decided so simply, and requires more comprehensive determinations and comparisons. Is truth-taking worth-taking? In worth-taking, the 'it values' does something *to me*, it pervades me. Being-true remains so to speak outside, I 'establish' it. In value-taking there is nothing theoretical; it has its own 'light', spreads its own illumination: '*lumen gloriae*'.

This objection may be extended to the entire foregoing critical analysis of teleological method, and it has – at the present point in the development of our problem – some apparent justification. Its refutation and radical overcoming, i.e. insight into its fundamental vacuity and 'bigotry', belong to the main content of the problematic towards which we are working. We concede the objection's validity, but, because we shall be dealing with it in more detail later, we shall not trouble ourselves with it now.

Another issue is more noteworthy. Supposing, it is said, that we may not fall back upon science and truth as cultural values – historically constituted forms – and we remain at the level of simple phenomena. The propositions are true, they are valid; because they are valid, they are acknowledged, and whatever is acknowledged [50] (or rejected) is always something of value. For this reason value must 'somehow' inhere in the judgement (*judgement as answer to a question*). Since we acknowledge truth, the latter must be something of value.

It will later become perfectly clear that, methodologically, only the fulfilled intuitive presentation is decisive. If, however, we take seriously the previously indicated objection, which rests essentially on deduction – with a simultaneous sudden introduction of a new value (validity) – this occurs because we are thus diverted into new contexts.

b) The Problem of Validity

The true proposition – in its content – does not exist in the manner of a house, but '*holds*, is valid'. What is actually meant with this word 'valid', which plays such an important role in contemporary philosophy, has until now not been discovered. It is a complicated problem because from the beginning it has been brought into relation with the phenomenon of value. Rickert says that the concept of validity is 'only scientifically useful . . . when one presupposes *values* which are valid . . . and which, as soon as they are related to a subject, stand over against this as an unconditional ought'.[11]

To unravel the problem of validity, it is crucial to keep it separate from the phenomenon of value. Whether value must be *presupposed* for validity is another question. To begin with, it depends on what validity as such means and in what kind of life-experience it is given. Does an originary kind of subject-correlate correspond to it, or is the former a founded or derivative, even highly derivative, phenomenon? As subject-correlate of validity or valid judgement, one could propose acknowledging or rejecting, [51] approval or disapproval. For a start, however, these two pairs of relations (position-taking) should not be made parallel. I can acknowledge something and at the same time disapprove of it. It is not the case that a 'yes' or 'no' as a genuine correlate of validating can always be demonstrated in a judgement. In the end, validity is a phenomenon constituted by its subject-matter, presupposing not only intersubjectivity but historical consciousness as such! Validity-taking, truth-taking, is not a position-taking [*Stellung-nehmen*]. Is the experience of validity founded upon a worth-taking? Or does it first of all found a declaration of value?

Is declaring a value constitutive for knowledge, or does validity announce itself as a value-free phenomenon in an ought which for its part *can*, but need not, found a declaration of value? Objectively expressed: is validity the primary possessor of value, and the ought something derivative? Or is value primary, validity and the ought derivative, so that the 'correlation of validating value and valuing subject' is, as Rickert says, the 'point of departure for all philosophy'?[12] Do value, and *practical* reason in the broadest sense, have genuine primacy, so that philosophy is the science of value? The teleological method presupposes that these important questions have already been resolved in the affirmative.

One thing is clear: a true proposition which 'is valid' does not give itself *as such* in a worth-taking. That does not rule out truth being a value, that is, being correctly declared as a value on the basis of a broad presupposed contexture of meaning. If so, then the conviction of the value-character of truth, presupposed in the function of giving ideals as an essential element of the teleological method, is justified, but only as a [52] *result* of complicated philosophical and scientific research. In other words: teleological method once again proves to be very much burdened by the problematic, presupposed as solved, towards whose solution it is itself supposed to assist.

It is evident, therefore, that teleological method does not come into consideration as the core of the method of primordial science. That does not exclude the possibility that it can acquire a meaning as a derivative *element* in a broader philosophical method.

Where do we stand? We are examining the suitability of teleological-critical method for primordial-scientific purposes. Since we do not have at our disposal secure and genuine criteria for a different method or fundamental viewpoint, the examination is possible only by way of a structural analysis.

The first thing to emerge was insight into the necessity of the founding function of material pregiving. It became clear that this creates and makes available a possible field of judging selectability for the principal function of method, namely the giving of ideals with its grounding critical judgement. The meaning of the giving of ideals, the content of the ideal itself, showed itself in terms of what, on the basis of the ideal, is to be achieved. In its enabling methodological core, teleological method presupposes the work it is to achieve; with its first meaningful step it is superfluous and the critique has already achieved its goal. Further analysis showed still new presuppositions and demonstrated the teleological method as laden with presuppositions: the phenomena of the ought, of providing the ought, of value and of worth-taking, the question of whether truth possesses value on the basis of an original worth-taking, or whether it is 'subsequently' declared as a value.

How does it come about that the structural analysis of the core function of teleological method brings to light this multiplicity of fundamental problems? The reason is [53] this method's claim to be primordial science; more precisely, the relation that it posits to the genuinely primordial-scientific *axiomatic problem*. Since the problem whose solution the teleological method is supposed to serve also proves to be truly primordial-scientific in nature (by way of the mark of circularity), it is possible, and even necessary, to undertake an analysis of all the functions of the teleological method, and regardless of the latter's inner impossibility.

c) The Relation between Material Pregiving and Ideal Giving. Being and the Ought

The analysis of the giving of ideals has been brought to a certain conclusion. The function of material pregivenness has likewise been explained and *above all defined in its scope*. There remains only the function linking these two, the function of critical normative selection of the genuine elements of normative thought. The specific kind of linkage is the critical judgement evaluating pregiven material on the basis of ideal givenness. This judgement, constantly measuring itself against the ideal, selects from the material just those formal elements that constitute the thought that corresponds to the ideal. The characteristic moments of norm fulfilment are not difficult to discover. *The value-judgement does not pose any special structural problem*, especially if ideal giving is presupposed as already executed and at our disposal. By this we mean that in its structure the value-judgement is *not significant for our problem*. In itself, however, it poses sufficient difficulties. (Separation of theoretical and a-theoretical value-judgements; their roles especially important at various points of complex founding contexts. The various modifications of judgements, depending on the substantive phenomena through which they are fulfilled.)

[54] It is, therefore, not the value-judgement itself, but rather what it presupposes as the possible foundations of its fulfilment, which is problematic. These presupposed foundations, however, are precisely the

two indicated functions of material and ideal givenness. In what way are these supposed once again to be problematic? What lies at the bottom of a possible judgement evaluating the material on the basis of the ideal? That the material stands under a norm which it ought to fulfil. A norm is something that ought to be, a value. The material is a Being [*Sein*], psychic Being. The norm is as such '*norm for*'; the norm character refers away from itself to something that it ought to fulfil. The norm as value refers to a Being [*ein Sein*].

How is such a reference possible? How do real psychic Being and an ideal ought become related to one another and comparable? Being and ought, i.e. Being and value, as two worlds fundamentally different in their basic structures, are separated from one another by a chasm. By means of the critical teleological method, it is the most noble intention of value philosophy to thoroughly expel everything connected with Being from the philosophical problematic, and to constitute the latter as a pure science of value. (On Rickert's 'third realm' and its phenomenal provenance in another context compare Rickert's interpretation of Being.[13]) A relational comparison of beings with beings is clearly possible; not, however, between Being and the ought, in respect of which spheres a comparative examination could establish only that they are essentially different, that is, without positive connection.

In its meaning, however, critical-teleological judgement presupposes such a connection, namely that material stands 'under' a norm, that a norm is 'norm for' a material. This presupposition, which is necessary for the meaningful fulfilment of a value-judgement, implies a positive substantive relation, [55] not merely the negative one of radical separation and incompatibility. At the same time, however, there is more in this presupposition than the idea of a positive relatedness between Being and the ought. *The character of relatedness is already determined.* This means that, for its part, the material as such refers beyond itself. It does not merely supply the subject-matter and then withdraw, playing no further role. Our characterization was therefore incomplete; it isolated the function of material giving and did not consider it 'in regard to' ideal giving. This 'in regard to' in the objective sense lies 'somehow' in the material, it extends to the ideal, just as for its part the norm is itself 'norm for something'. This mutual relatedness of pregiven material and norm, with the entire complex of problems contained therein, was not yet perceived as a problem. The proponents of teleological method are, so to speak, fascinated by the radical division between Being and value, and do not notice that they have only theoretically broken the bridges between the two spheres, and now stand helpless on one of the banks.

Material as pregiven field of selection and the ideal as critical norm once again become a problem in respect of their possible connection. Not only is the structure of this connection problematic, but, as a deeper analysis will show, so also is the nature of the overarching unity of the two.

The relational state of affairs presupposed in a potential critical value-judgement that remains unnoticed and unexamined is characterized from the side of the ideal as 'norm for', and from the side of the material as 'under the norm', 'normative', 'norm-related'. In order to clarify this connection, let us look at the material in a methodological context.

The analysis of material pregivenness up to this point has shown that it makes material available, [56] providing the field and ground for critical normative judgement. We restricted ourselves to theoretical knowledge, in accordance with our point of departure in the complex of the particular sciences. This method itself posits, as guiding norm, truth as absolutely valid value. In relation to this normative ideal for theoretical knowing, material giving provides psychic processes of knowledge for which the appropriate necessary conditions of genuine norm fulfilment are to be found. This methodological orientation to a possible discovery of the relevant moments of psychic cognitive processes *presupposes that the latter are unambiguously characterized,* at least to the extent that precisely the sought-after moments become visible. How far the characterization of psychical cognitive processes to be fulfilled in material giving needs to extend can be determined by clearly marking off the totality of moments that come into consideration as norms. For this, however, these moments would have to be known in advance. But if this were known, then the whole further arrangement of the method would again be superfluous. Not possessing this knowledge, we want to arrive at it. It is, therefore, not enough to develop the pregiving psychological characterization only up to a certain distance; it is necessary for material pregivenness to characterize psychic phenomena in their full scope. Otherwise there remains the ineradicable possibility of omissions. Moments that from the point of view of the norm come unconditionally into question simply could not be given. The function of material pregivenness is not free, but is subservient and methodologically bound by its functional meaning in the entire method. The guarantee of a perfect characteriza-tion, free from all obscurity, is in this sense a co-requisite. It is, therefore, a complete misunderstanding of the genuine meaning of the method [57] advocated by Windelband when he says that rough characterizations are sufficient.

Let us assume, however, that psychology has given a perfect character-ization of knowledge processes and by means of thoroughly researched factual knowledge provided a solid foundation for critical value-judgement, such that all windy speculation and construction is kept at bay. Factual psychological knowledge rests on empirical experience; every proposition is authenticated through experience, through precise determination and comparative description of what is given, and through location within the likewise empirically grounded lawfulness of the cog-nitive process. Empirical sciences are in-ductive, proceeding from one item of empirical knowledge to another, always leading from what has already been attained to new knowledge, higher comparisons and general laws. Therefore empirical sciences can never be completed, not only in the sense that there is always the possibility that hitherto unknown facts will be discovered, but also in so far as there will be new hitherto unseen sides to previously known facts already ordered within general laws, sides that were inaccessible to the previous methods. The empirical sciences possess a hypothetical kind of validity – *if* the empirically established ground is assumed and no new experience subverts this, *then* such and such a law pertains, i.e. is valid: *if – then*. The empirical sciences as such can never dispense with this *if*; it attaches itself to them like an inhibiting and burdensome weight, or, more precisely expressed in the same simile, these sciences have weight in themselves, as experience they are *heavy* – and on account of this heaviness they always sink back into the hypothetical and preliminary, are never absolutely secure.

We see that the genuine sense of the teleological method requires for its possible fulfilment the complete characterization of material giving. There are two reasons why psychology as empirical science [58] cannot meet this requirement. As an empirical science it never attains completion in its content. But in addition, what it establishes about this content has merely hypothetical or provisional validity, *dependent* on other cases *not* subverting it. Material giving is necessary for the method, and so psychology is taken up. But empirical psychology never gets beyond hypothetical provisionality and relative validity. It is supposed to be the foundation of primordial-scientific method, which would establish in primordial-scientific fashion the conditions of true knowledge, and as such would ground these conditions, which would hold (be valid) not only in this or that situation but *absolutely*. The foundation of critical value-judgement is constantly shifting, and with it the house of philosophy that is built upon it!

We must immerse ourselves, with the highest degree of clarity, in this lability of the fact and factual knowledge, of the *factum*, until it is unmistakable in its givenness.

We worked previously with the idea of a possible psychology as a rigorous empirical science with a unified, methodologically secured fund of established knowledge. In fact not even this exists, but rather a rich confusion of various psychological theories and methods, a wealth of particular results which through further methodological processing are again transformed. If it is honest, the critical method finds itself in profound bewilderment, which cannot be overcome by reaching out for a convenient and (for some momentary purpose) plausible psychological cognition and – undisturbed by its scientific 'value' – going on to philosophize and to outline the system of values (to be illustrated by 'psychological theories of judgement').

§ 12. Inclusion of the Pre-Theoretical Sphere. Psychology's Sphere of Objects [59]

Let us further extend the scope of our problematic. So far we have restricted ourselves to the theoretical sphere. For its part material giving was likewise limited to psychical processes of knowledge.

There are a number of reasons for the effective restriction to the theoretical sphere. First of all, one believes that the elements of norm and form can be exposed *most easily* in this domain. Scientific thought, where the theoretical is concentrated bodily, has the character of secure accessibility and objectivity. The factually existing and already developed sciences contain a clearly definable deposit of theoretical knowledge.

Accordingly, one also assumes that the norms and forms obtained in this domain are easiest to ground. The idea of *truth* as value in particular has the character of universal validity, while the moral ideal, and still more the aesthetic ideal, is subject to great variations in conception and formulation.

Further, preference for the theoretical is grounded in the conviction that this is the basic level that grounds all other spheres in a specific way and that is manifested when one speaks, for example, of moral, artistic, or religious 'truth'. The theoretical, one says, colours all other domains of value, and it does this all the more obviously in so far as it is itself conceived as a value. This primacy of the theoretical must be broken, but not in order to proclaim the primacy of the practical, and not in order to introduce something that shows the problems from a new side, but because the theoretical itself and as such refers back to something pre-theoretical.

[60] If material giving also extends to unknown psychic processes, then, since these phenomena find themselves in an even more impoverished state in regard to their experience, the methodological character of psychology becomes even more problematic.

In this way we come to the *object-sphere* of psychology in general. For what is the psychic as such? In what way are precisely *these beings* supposed to be subject to norms and to realize an ought? *What is the psychic?*

Does this question point in the direction of our problem, or does it stray into an isolated region of a special theory of science? We are now no longer posing the question in relation to a specific region of Being, but since everything either *is* psychic or is mediated *through* the psychic, the concept of material giving has the greatest possible breadth. The method itself, and above all *those* phenomena that we have exhibited in the complex structure of the giving of ideals, belong in the psychic and become possible data in its preliminary function. Our problematic concentrates itself so to speak on a single point, it centres itself in the material giving, more precisely in the question of how the psychic is to be given as a sphere. Included in this is also the question of how the phenomena of ideal giving are to be given. (Historical excursus on the development of psychology.)

Can this total sphere be known in any other way than through hypothetical-inductive empirical knowledge? Is there a way of considering the psychic which allows for the solution of primordial-scientific problems? Can the psychic itself show objective levels that constitute the domain of objects of primordial science? More concretely, can the axiomatic problems, the questions concerning the ultimate norms of knowing, willing and feeling, be demonstrated in the psychic itself? Do I stand in the psychic as in a primordial sphere? Is the genuine origin or 'primal spring' [*Ur-sprung*] to be found here? [61] Can anything at all 'spring from' [*ent-springen*] the psychic, come to a 'leap' [*Sprung*] in it?

The Being of the psychic, in psychology's sense, is not at rest but in constant change. It is a continuity of processes flowing in time and characterized precisely by temporality. This sphere of occurrences does not fill up space, is not analysable into elementary processes, and does not consist of basic facts to be dissolved like elementary pieces of beings (sensations, representations). The piecing together into higher processes is governed by the laws of the psychic occurrence itself, laws which thus in turn explain the psychic in its being so and so [*Sosein*]. Atomizing analysis discovers in the constructive consideration of laws its counter-movement towards the unity of the total sphere, which displays the unity of a complex of subject-matter that itself can be brought into material relation with the matter of the psychic complex. The sphere of subject-matter as such can be attained only through pure dedication to the subject-matter [*Sache*]. All obfuscation of the material sphere through unproven and arbitrary theorems and preconceptions must be avoided. What is appropriate in a sphere of subject-matter [*Sachsphäre*] is only a 'description' that exhibits facts. I do not, through description, depart from this sphere, and when it is the sphere of primordiality so much more closely does description remain attached to it. Description does not tolerate anything that alters or re-forms the subject-matter. But how is something like a science supposed to be possible by way of an ever ongoing serial description that always begins anew? Does description as such ever come to an end? Does not whatever is described remain behind, always escaping the descriptive context? And is there in any case a possible starting-point for description? Description itself is surely a psychic phenomenon and thus itself belongs to the sphere of the material thing. What is that supposed to mean, that one thing [*Sache*] describes another? Is description as such a form of connection between things? Perhaps the serial after- and next-to-one-another is just such a connection.

[62] Is there even a single thing when there are only things? Then there would be no thing at all; not even *nothing*, because with the sole supremacy of the sphere of things there is not even the 'there is' [*es gibt*]. Is there the 'there is'?

PART TWO

Phenomenology as Pre-Theoretical Primordial Science [63]

CHAPTER ONE
Analysis of the Structure of Experience

§ 13. The Experience of the Question: 'Is There Something?'

Already in the opening of the question 'Is there . . . ?' there is something. Our *entire* problematic has arrived at a crucial point, which, however, appears insignificant and even miserly. Everything depends on understanding and following this insignificance in its pure meaning, on fastening on to it and no longer thinking back to teleological method, ideal and material giving, psychical totality, material domain of things, and indeed – even especially so – the idea of primordial science and its method. We are standing at the methodological cross-road which will decide on the very life or death of philosophy. We stand at an abyss: either into nothingness, that is, absolute reification, pure thingness, or we somehow leap into *another world*, more precisely, we manage for the first time to make the leap [*Sprung*] into the world as such.

a) The Psychic Subject

We now know that a comprehensible series of problems and questions has led us to this insignificant and miserly question. If we forget this road, we deny our provenance *and ourselves*. If *we* were not at all first here, [64] then there would be no such question. It is clear, therefore, that in the entire course of our deliberation we have withheld an essential element whose timely incorporation would have structured our problematic differently. We have not even arrived at the psychic totality in its completeness. We spoke of psychic processes without a common binding core, and of knowledge processes without a psychic subject in which these run their course. We moved within the insuperable perplexities of a 'psychology without soul'. It is by no means necessary that we should lose ourselves in metaphysics and think of the soul as substance, but we must round off the psychic context by way of its relation to the psychic subject. In this way the object and subject-matter of psychology will be complete and the difficulties resolved.

A psychic process in itself, isolated as a thing, explains nothing. Psychic processes like sensations, perceptions and memories, are explained as cognitive processes only when they occur in a *psychic subject which* knows. In this way bridges are now also made between psychic objects and the psychic subject, and the cognitive process is traced back to its origin.

Does this new positioning of the problem, presented *in this way*, bring us anything essentially new? Does the psychic subject explain anything? The material context of the psychic has certainly arrived at a point of unity of the subject-matter, but basically we have not left the material sphere. The problem has only been shifted within the psychic context of the subject-matter. Knowing as a psychic process is in no way explained when I acknowledge it as occurring in a psychic subject. One thing is put in relation to another thing, one psychic thing is connected to another, [65] but the material context of the psychic itself is still highly problematic. What is it supposed to mean that one psychic thing is in another, and establishes a connection with something external to it? We are thrown from one thing to another, which like any thing remains mute.

We have made a hasty diversion, hoping to find a saving anchor in the neglected psychic subject. Once again we have given in to a stubborn habit of thought, without it occurring to us to explore the simple sense of the trivial question 'Is there something?' This question was deliberately chosen in order to minimize pre-judgements.

It was a restless disjointed course from one multiplicity of problems to another, a way which became ever more empty, finally dwindling to the barren question of a material context and its knowledge. We have gone into the aridity of the desert, hoping, instead of always *knowing* things, to intuit understandingly and to *understand intuitively*: ' . . . and the Lord God let the *tree of life* grow up *in the middle of the garden* – and the tree of knowledge of good and evil' (Genesis 2: 9).

b) The Interrogative Comportment. Various Senses of the 'There is'

We wish to respond to the simple sense of the question, to understand what it implies. It is a matter of sounding out the motives from which it lives. The question is lived, is experienced [*erlebt*]. I experience. I experience something vitally. When we simply give ourselves over to this experience, we know nothing of a process passing before us [*Vor-gang*], or of an occurrence. Neither anything physical nor anything psychic is given. But one could immediately object: the experience is a process in me, in my soul, therefore obviously something psychic. Let us look at it carefully. [66] This objection is not to the point, because it already reifies the experience rather than taking it as such, as it gives itself. No misunderstanding must creep into the word 'motive'. To hear out motives does not mean to search out causes of emergence or reifying conditions [*Be-dingungen*], it does not mean to search out things which explain the experience in a thingly way and within a thingly context. We must understand the pure motives of the sense of the pure experience.

The term 'lived experience' [*Erlebnis*] is today so faded and worn thin that, if it were not so fitting, it would be best to leave it aside. Since it cannot be avoided, it is all the more necessary to understand its essence.

In asking 'Is there something?' I comport myself by setting something, indeed anything whatsoever, before me as questionable. Let us here leave aside entirely the moment of questionability: 'I comport myself.'

'I comport myself' – is this contained in the sense of the experience? Let us enact the experience with full vividness and examine its sense. To be sure, it would be no ill-conceived reification and substantification of the lived experience if I said that it contained something like 'I comport myself'. But what is decisive is that simple inspection [*Hinsehen*] does not discover anything like an 'I'. What I see is just that 'it lives' [*es lebt*], moreover that it lives towards something, that it is directed towards something by way of questioning, something that is itself questionable. What do 'questioning' and 'questionability' mean? Already here we are temporarily at a limit. What is the sense of the questioning comportment? If I bring this experience to givenness in its full sense and meaningful motives, can the essence of 'questionable' and 'questionability' be understood in an appropriate way? It is tempting to interpret the comportment of questioning in relation to a sought-after answer. Questioning comportment is motivated, one might say, by a desire to know. [67] It arises from a drive for knowledge which itself originates from θαυμάζειν,

ANALYSIS OF THE STRUCTURE OF EXPERIENCE

astonishment and wonder.[1] If we were now to follow such interpretations and 'explanations', we would have to turn away from the simple sense of the experience; we would have to abandon the idea of holding on clearly to just what is given to us. We would have to venture into new and problematic contexts which would necessarily endanger the unadulterated authenticity of simple analysis. Let us therefore remain with the sense of the lived experience as such, keeping a firm hold on what it gives. It also gives that which, just on its own (in respect of questioning and questionability), cannot ultimately be understood. This is its ownmost meaning [*Eigen-sinn*] which it cannot explain by itself.

In this experience *something* is questioned in relation to anything whatsoever. The questioning has a definite content: whether '*there is*' a something, that is the question. The 'there is' [*es geben*] stands in question, or, more accurately, stands in questioning. It is not asked whether something moves or rests, whether something contradicts itself, whether something works, whether something exists, whether something values, whether something ought to be, but rather whether *there is* something. What does 'there is' mean?

There are numbers, there are triangles, there are Rembrandt paintings, there are submarines. I say that 'there is' still rain today, that tomorrow 'there is' roast veal. A multiplicity of 'there is', each time with a different meaning, but in each case with an identical moment of meaning. Also this utterly flaccid meaning of 'there is', so to speak emptied of particular meanings, has precisely on account of its simplicity its manifold puzzles. Where can we find the meaningful motive for the meaning of 'there is'? Once again a new element of meaning refers the question and its content (there is) beyond itself.

It is asked whether there is *something*. It is not asked whether there are tables or chairs, houses or trees, sonatas [68] by Mozart or religious powers, but whether there is *anything whatsoever*. What does 'anything whatsoever' mean? Something universal, one might say, indeed the most universal of all, applying to any possible object whatsoever. To say of something that it is something is the minimum assertion I can make about it. I stand over against it without presuppositions. And yet: the meaning of 'something', primitive as it appears to be, shows itself in accord with its sense as motivator of a whole process of motivations. This is already suggested by the fact that, in attempting to grasp the meaning of 'something in general', we return to individual objects with particular concrete content. Perhaps this reversion is necessary. In the final analysis it belongs to the meaning of 'something in general' to relate to something concrete, whereby the meaningful character of this 'relating' still remains problematic.

c) The Role of the Questioner

It was said above that the characterization which reads an '*I* comport *myself*' into the simple experience of the question is inappropriate and inapplicable, because in immediate observation I do not find anything like an 'I', but only an 'ex-perience [*Er-leben*] of something', a '*living towards something*'.

It will be objected that an 'I' does indeed belong to the sense of the question, i.e. that 'there is' means that it is given there, *for me the questioner*. Let us again immerse ourselves in the lived experience. Does this contain any kind of meaningful reference back to I myself, with this particular name and this age, I who stand here at the lectern? Examine the matter for yourself. Does there lie in the question 'Is there something?' a for me (Dr X) – a for me (candidate of philosophy, Y) – a for me (student of jurisprudence, Z)? Clearly not. Therefore, not only is no 'I' *immediately* apprehended, but in broadening out the sphere of intuition, thus [69] abandoning any restriction to precisely *myself*, it is evident that the experience has no relation to any individual 'I'. Precisely because the question relates in general to *an* 'I', it is without relation to *my* 'I'. These two phenomena necessarily motivate each other. *Just because the sense of the experience is without relation to my 'I' (to me as so and so), the still somehow necessary 'I' and I-relation are not seen in simple inspection.* As we shall show, this proposition is no mere tautology.

Yet the experience *is*, even when I avoid every kind of reification and insertion into a reifying context. It has a *now*, it is there – and is even somehow *my* experience. I am there with it, I experience it vitally, it belongs to *my* life, but it is still so detached from me in its sense, so absolutely far from the 'I', so absolutely '*I*-remote' [*Ich-fern*].

I ask: 'Is there something?' The 'is there' is a 'there is' for an 'I', and yet it is not *I* to and for *whom* the question relates.

A wealth of quite new problem-connections is loosened up: problems to be sure, but on the other hand matters of immediate intuition that point to new contextures of meaning. However simply and primitively the interrogative experience gives itself, in respect of all its components it is peculiarly dependent. Nevertheless, from this experience a ground-laying and essential insight can now be achieved. (Characterization of the lived experience as event [*Er-eignis*] – meaningful, not thing-like.)

Whatever course the further analysis might take, whatever questions might arise in respect of the analysis and its nature, it is crucial to see that we are not dealing with a reified context, and that the object of our examination is not merely an actually existing occurrence. The question is whether there is an object here at all. The living out of ex-perience is not a thing that exists in brute fashion, beginning and ceasing to be like a process [*Vor-gang*] passing by before us. The 'relating to' is not a thing-like part, to which some other thing, [70] the 'something', is attached. The living and the lived of experience are not joined together in the manner of existing objects.

From this particular experience, the non-thingly character of all experiences whatsoever can be brought to full intuitive understanding.

§ 14. The Environmental Experience

We wish, however, and not simply for the sake of easing our understanding, to bring to mind a second experience, which to begin with stands in a certain contrast to the first. Bringing this contrast into view will at the same time advance the direction of our problem.

The content of the first experience, of the question 'Is there something?', resulted from following the assumption of a single exclusive reified context as existent (absolutization of thingliness). That could give the impression that the current state of our problematic prescribes a different experience for the purpose of analysis. This is not the case, and that it does not need to be the case, that there is rather a definite possibility of drawing every experience into the analysis as an example, makes itself plain. But this realm of selectability extends only to *my* experiences, the experiences that *I* have and *I* have had.

If we admit this, we add to our 'presuppositions' a very crude one. *I* bring a new experience to givenness not only for myself, but I ask you all, each isolated I-self who is sitting here, to do the same. Indeed we wish to a certain degree to enter into a unitary experience. You come as usual into this lecture-room at the usual hour and go to *your* usual place. Focus on this experience of 'seeing *your* place', [71] or you can in turn put yourselves in my own position: coming into the lecture-room, I see the lectern. We dispense with a verbal formulation of this. What do 'I' see? Brown surfaces, at right angles to one another? No, I see something else. A largish box with another smaller one set upon it? Not at all. I see the lectern at which I am to speak. You see the lectern, from which you are to be addressed, and from where I have spoken to you previously. In pure experience there is no 'founding' interconnection, as if I first of all see intersecting brown surfaces, which then reveal themselves to me as a box, then as a desk, then as an academic lecturing desk, a lectern, so that I attach lectern-hood to the box like a label. All that is simply bad and misguided interpretation, diversion from a pure seeing into the experience. I see the lectern in one fell swoop, so to speak, and not in isolation, but as adjusted a bit too high for me. I see – and immediately so – a book lying upon it as annoying to me (a book, not a collection of layered pages with black marks strewn upon them), I see the lectern in an orientation, an illumination, a background.

Certainly, you will say, that might be what happens in immediate experience, for me and in a certain way also for you, for you also see this complex of wooden boards *as* a lectern. This object, which all of us here perceive, somehow has the specific meaning 'lectern'. It is different if a farmer from deep in the Black Forest is led into the lecture-room. Does he see the lectern, or does he see a box, an arrangement of boards? He sees 'the place for the teacher', he sees the object as fraught with meaning. If someone saw a box, then he would not be seeing a piece of wood, a thing, a natural object. But consider a Negro from Senegal suddenly transplanted here from his hut. What he would see, gazing at this object, [72] is difficult to say precisely: perhaps something to do with magic, or something behind which one could find good protection against arrows and flying stones. Or would he not know what to make of it at all, just seeing complexes of colours and surfaces, simply a thing, a something which simply is? So my seeing and that of a Senegal Negro are fundamentally different. All they have in common is that in both cases something is seen. *My* seeing is to a high degree something individual, which I certainly may not – without further ado – use to ground the analysis of the experience. For this analysis is supposed to yield universally valid scientific results in conjunction with the elaboration of the problem.

Assuming that the experiences were fundamentally different, and that only my experience existed, I still assert that universally valid propositions are possible. This implies that these sentences would also be valid for the experience of the Senegal Negro. Let us put this assertion to one side, and focus once again on the experience of the Senegal Negro. Even if he saw the lectern simply as a bare something that is there, it would have a meaning for him, a moment of signification. There is, however, the possibility of showing that the assumption of the transplanted unscientific (not culture-less) Negro seeing the lectern as simply something is non-sensical but not contradictory, i.e. not impossible in a formal-*logical* sense. The Negro will see the lectern much more as something 'which he does not know what to make of'. The meaningful character of 'instrumental strangeness', and the meaningful character of the 'lectern', are in their essence absolutely identical.

In the experience of seeing the lectern something is given *to me* from out of an immediate environment [*Umwelt*]. This environmental milieu (lectern, book, blackboard, notebook, fountain pen, caretaker, student fraternity, tram-car, motor-car, etc.) does not consist just of things, objects, which are then [73] conceived as meaning this and this; rather, the meaningful is primary and immediately given to me without any mental detours across thing-oriented apprehension. Living in an environment, it signifies to me everywhere and always, everything has the character of world. It is everywhere the case that '*it worlds*' [*es weltet*], which is something different from 'it values' [*es wertet*]. (The problem of the connection between the two belongs to the eidetic genealogy of primary motivations and leads into difficult problem spheres.)

§ 15. Comparison of Experiential Structures. Process and Event

Let us again recall the environmental experience, my seeing of the lectern. Do I find in the pure sense of the experience, in my comportment on seeing the lectern, giving itself environmentally, anything like an 'I'? In this experiencing, in this living-towards, there is something of me: *my* 'I' goes out beyond itself and resonates *with* this seeing, as does the 'I' of the Negro in his own experience of 'something which *he* cannot make out'. *More precisely*: only through the accord of this particular 'I' does it experience something environmental, where we can say that 'it worlds'. Wherever and whenever 'it worlds' for me, *I* am somehow there. Now consider the experience of the question 'Is there something?' I do not find myself in this. The 'anything whatsoever', about whose 'there is' I ask, does not 'world'. The worldly is here extinguished, and we grasp every potential environing world as 'anything whatsoever'. This grasping, this firm fixing of the object as such, occurs at the cost of forcing back my own 'I'. It belongs to the meaning of 'anything whatsoever' that in its determination *I do not* as such come into accord with it: this resonating, this going out of myself, is prevented. The object, being an object as such, does not touch *me*. The 'I' that firmly fixes is no longer *I myself*. The firm fixing as an experience is still only a rudiment of [74] vital experience; it is a de-vivification [*Ent-leben*]. What is objectified, what is known, is as such re-moved [*ent-fernt*], lifted out of the actual experience. The objective occurrence, the happening as objectified and known, we describe as a *process*; it simply passes before my knowing 'I', to which it is related only by being-known, i.e. in a flaccid I-relatedness reduced to the miminum of life-experience. It is in the nature of the thing and thing-contexture to give themselves only in knowledge, that is, only in theoretical comport- ment and for the theoretical 'I'. In the theoretical comportment I am directed to something, but *I* do not live (as historical 'I') towards this or that worldly element. Let us once again contrast entire contexts of experi- ence, so that it does not appear that the 'opposition' pertains only to isolated experiences.

Let us place ourselves into the comportment of the astronomer, who in astrophysics investigates the phenomenon of sunrise simply as a process in nature before which he is basically indifferent, and on the other hand the experience of the chorus of Theban elders, which in Sophocles' *Antigone* looks at the rising sun on the first friendly morning after a successful defensive battle:

> ἀκτὶς ἀελίου, τὸ κάλ-
> λιστον ἐππαπύλω φανὲν
> Θήβα τῶν προτέρων φάος

> Thou most beautiful glance of the sun,
> That upon seven-gated Thebes
> So long shines . . .[2]

[75] This contrast does not solve but only initially poses the problem of the *how* of different modes of experience. But for the time being it will suffice for our purposes. How do we see the experiences? The questions of how such seeing is possible, of what it itself is, and whether it is not also theory (it is, after all, supposed to become science), will be set aside for the moment. Let us try to understand both experiences and see if we can regard them as processes, as objects which are re-presented, firmly fixed

before us. But something does happen. In seeing the lectern I am fully present in my 'I'; it resonates with the experience, as we said. It is an experience proper to me and so do I see it. However, it is not a process but rather an *event of appropriation* [*Ereignis*] (non-process, in the experience of the question a residue of this event). Lived experience does not pass in front of me like a thing, but I appropriate [*er-eigne*] it to myself, and it appropriates [*er-eignet*] itself according to its essence. If I understand it in this way, then I understand it not as process, as thing, as object, but in a quite new way, as an event of appropriation. Just as little as I see something thing-like do I see an objectivated sphere of things, a Being, neither physical nor psychical Being. Attending strictly to the experience, I do not see anything psychical. Event of appropriation is not to be taken as if I appropriate the lived experience to myself from outside or from anywhere else; 'outer' and 'inner' have as little meaning here as 'physical' and 'psychical'. The experiences are events of appropriation in so far as they live out of one's 'own-ness', and life lives only in this way. (With this the event-like essence of appropriation is still not fully determined.)

Granted that I could make clear that my experiences are of a distinctive character, and are not thing-like or object-like beings, this evidence would have validity only for [76] me and my experiences. How is a science supposed to be built upon this? Science is knowledge and knowledge has objects. Science determines and fixes objects in an objective manner. A science of experiences would have to objectify experiences and thus strip away their non-objective character as lived experience and event of appropriation.

Already when I speak of *two* of my experiences I have objectified them: the one and the other, both are a something. For every experience that I want to consider I must isolate and lift out, break up and destroy the contexture of the experience so that in the end and despite all efforts to the contrary, I have only a heap of things.

Chapter Two
The Problem of Presuppositions [77]

---

§ 16. The Epistemological Question of the Reality of the External World.
Standpoints of Critical Realism and Idealism

But perhaps all these difficulties can be overcome. Let us assume, to begin with, that proceeding from a subjective and individual sphere of lived experience we can construct a science that does not treat experience in an objectified manner. There is one thing that cannot be overcome, namely the presupposition of the experiences themselves. Under these conditions there are experiences that are laden in greater or lesser degree with further presuppositions. May I therefore without further ado presuppose these as given? This is disputed.[1] Let us again bring to mind the two oft-mentioned experiences: of the question 'Is there something?' and of the lectern.

In the question 'Is there something?' nothing at all is presupposed. What is asked is whether 'there is' something, not whether something exists, occurs, values, worlds. Such an experience may be rare, but it is still an experience. The greater part and certainly the entire fullness of environmental experiences is heavily laden with presuppositions. Does my environing world really exist? Is it so obvious that the external world is real and not rather only my representation, my lived experience? How shall this be decided? I cannot simply resolve to adopt one or another epistemological conception. [78] Is it (critical) realism that is correct, or transcendental philosophy? Aristotle or Kant? How is this 'burning' question of the reality of the external world to be solved?

The question is 'burning' because it inhibits every step forward, because it is constantly there in its appeal to the critical consciousness. Every environmental experience is affected by it, not only the existence and reality of the impersonal environmental elements, but in particular the personal, human beings and their experiences. Upon the reality of the latter everything depends, if, that is, a universal science of experience is to have any meaning. If the experiences of other subjects have reality at all, then this can only be as proper events of appropriation [*Er-eignisse*], and they can only be evident as such events, i.e. as appropriated by an historical 'I'. For me they are not events, for according to their nature they can be so only for another. The procedure whereby through external perception of the human body I come to inner processes, then to essentially non-eventlike lived experiences, from these to another 'I' and then across the I-experience to events, is quite complicated. Furthermore, it is not only a question of the reality of isolated 'Is', but of groups, communities, societies, church, state. These are not bare abstract concepts. The empirical sciences, historical science as also the natural sciences, are constructed upon the reality of the external world.

At this point one might decide provisionally to leave aside all those experiences that posit the real as real, and to investigate just the others. But basically nothing is achieved by this. For I must still go out beyond my own 'I' and find a way to reality, or else declare the latter a fiction. So what is required is that I make a clean slate of it and strip the problem of its constantly disruptive impact. But one difficulty still remains. The problem is an epistemological one [79], or one could almost say: the question of the reality of the external world is *the* problem of epistemology, of the basic discipline of philosophy whose idea we are in the first place seeking. If we now take up this problem we are presupposing epistemology and its way of questioning. In order to strip away the presuppositions of environmental experience (assumption of the reality of the external world), to which we are limiting, and for good reasons can limit, ourselves, we make other presuppositions.

You will have no doubt noticed that from the moment where we entered into the sphere of experiences, we gave up the critical attitude with regard to a formal conceptual analysis, and devoted ourselves purely to our own sphere. Similarly, from this point onwards, the former anxious avoidance of any kind of 'presuppositions' ceases. Precisely at this stage, where we are steering towards the centre of the problematic, it is not at all a matter of making 'presuppositions'. A peculiar preparation for entering into primordial science!

So we are practising epistemology, but with the assurance – for our own sake and for the sake of the strict demands of genuine method – of eventually 'justifying' this presupposition. We distil from the diverse and almost unsurveyable problematic of the reality of the external world two typical attempts at a solution: Aristotle and Kant. To be sure, I am treating more their modern expressions, without losing myself in details.

Who is right? Aristotle, Kant, or neither? What is the contemporary solution? Can it only be a compromise?

Common to both solutions is, first of all, the claim to be *critical*. The attitude in which I naively live within my environing world – for example, the experience I have of the lectern – is prescientific and epistemologically untested. The naive person who knows nothing of philosophical criticism, [80] to whom rigorous methodological inquiry is quite foreign, does not understand the necessity for critically examining his perceptions.

Epistemology arouses us out of this slumber and points to problems. These cannot be seen by clinging to immediate life-experience. One must rise to the critical standpoint. One must be free and able, in a progressive age of reason and culture, to place oneself over oneself. In this way one enters a new dimension, the philosophical.

If, from this standpoint, I consider the experience of the lectern, it is clear that what is primarily given are sensations, *initially optical* ones, or, if I simultaneously come into physical contact with the lectern, sensations of *touch. These data of sense are given.* Up to this point the two basic epistemological standpoints, critical *realism* and critical-transcendental *idealism*, are in agreement. But now they go off in opposed directions, posing the epistemological question in different ways.

Critical realism asks: how do I get out of the 'subjective sphere' of sense data to knowledge of the external world?

Critical-transcendental idealism poses the problem: how, remaining within the 'subjective sphere', do I arrive at objective knowledge?

Both standpoints bind themselves to the most securely grounded factual sciences, namely the natural sciences, but, corresponding to their different epistemological problematics, they do so in different ways. In particular, their respective conceptions of the 'subjective sphere' are fundamentally different.

As mentioned, the point of departure is the existence of sense data. This gives rise to the obvious question of where they come from and how they are caused. A blind person has no optical sensations, [81] a deaf person no acoustical ones. Such sensations depend on the existence of functioning organs. Physiology provides extensive information on this matter, not only concerning the individual organs, but on the nerve-pathways proceeding from them, and on the central nervous system. The sense organs give rise to sensations only when they are stimulated from outside, as effects of external causes. Physics provides additional crucial information: brown is not really in the lectern; the sensory qualities, colours, tones, etc., are in their nature subjective. Only the movements of various wavelengths in the ether are objectively real. But what is initially of decisive importance is that there exists a real external world. The sense data are indeed qualitatively different from their objective stimulants, but in no way are they pure products of subjectivity. The world is not merely my representation, but really exists independently outside my subjectivity. The world is not just appearance, but I know it. Physics is an irrefutable *demonstratio ad oculos* of its objective existence.

Knowledge of the thing-in-itself: the only difficulty with this epistemological conception consists in the relation between the central nervous system (i.e. the brain) and the soul, between physiological and psychical processes. But today there are well-grounded theories for the removal of this difficulty: the standpoint of psycho-physical parallelism on the one hand, and the hypothesis of causal connection on the other. Critical realism today also attracts followers outside the Aristotelian-Scholastic philosophy. Its main achievement stems from *Külpe*.

I know not only the reality of natural objects, but the reality of other human beings. The latter are also given to me initially through sense data, through expressive movements determined by physiological processes, which, however, themselves arise from psychic processes, [82] from a psychic contexture that I conceive unitarily as soul, subject, another 'I'. Epistemologically I go along the same path as from sense data and subjectivity to reality, only in the opposite direction.

The theory of critical realism is self-contained; it has the advantage of avoiding speculative constructions and holding fast to the facts, to the rigorous scientific insights of physics and physiology. It grants the reality of the external world and teaches the possibility of knowing the things in themselves.

We can clarify the problematic of critical idealism by likewise proceeding from sense data, but in the other direction. The sense data are data only for a subject, for an 'I' ; they are data only in so far as we are *conscious* of them. What kind of function do they have in knowing beings? Just that the data get eliminated. They are the X of the knowledge equation that is to be solved. Let us again attend to the facts of natural science, in particular of physics. Mathematical natural science originated when Galileo inquired not into the causes of realities, but into the objectively valid laws of natural occurrences, independently of (bad) subjectivity. Closer examination reveals that natural science, physics, discovers laws not through description of sense data, but through their resolution (infinitesimal calculus) and ordering within contextures of movement. This treatment of sense data, their ordered insertion within processes of movement, the concepts of these orderly movements, mathematics in its function as an indispensable tool: these are all achievements of thought, more precisely of its meaning, of the objectively valid forms of thought.

[83] The objectivity and real validity of knowledge are not obtained, as realism believes, by searching out the causes of sensations. For this searching out is itself thought, which can be realized only through the transformation of sense data with the help of logical forms, i.e. the categories, to which causality also belongs. However, what constitutes objective knowledge is not my individual thought processes, but the total system of categories and principles as discovered and validated by epistemology. Objectivity and reality are correlates of consciousness as such, of the epistemological subject as such. All Being is only in and through thought, and all thought is thought of Being. For idealism too the world is not mere representation, but reality is always what it is only as we are *conscious* of it; there are only objects as objects of consciousness, and genuine reality is the objectivity of the sciences. Only what becomes objective in scientific knowledge is real in the genuine sense.

Which solution is genuine, which standpoint is correct? To come to a decision, one could try to submit the competing arguments of both directions to a critical examination. Such a critical survey of opinions and counter-opinions would not only be out of keeping with the economy of this lecture-course, but it would not be nearly so helpful as one might presume. Fundamentally, we are subjecting both standpoints to critical questioning.

The solution of transcendental philosophy as expressed in the objective idealism of the Marburg school, upon which we based the above sketch, shows a basic defect: the one-sided, absolutizing restriction of knowledge and its object, therefore the concept of reality, to mathematical natural science. Initially, [84] however, this is not a decisive objection, for it may well be that precisely through this restriction epistemology solves the problem with a depth and an exactness not previously attained. Nevertheless, the Marburg school's narrowing of the concept of knowledge is of *fundamental* significance for us.

Critical realism is superior with respect to the scope of its problematic. It poses the problem of the reality of the external world as such, but solves it with the assistance of insights from the real sciences, whose very right to posit reality has to be explained.

Both directions have some sort of relation to mathematical natural science. Idealism presupposes this science simply as a fact which it then seeks to know in its logical structure. Realism takes this science as a fact, but at the same time as the means of explanation and solution of its problem. In both cases a problem in which theoretical knowledge is itself in question. Moreover, this question is itself to be resolved by theoretical means.

§ 17. The Primacy of the Theoretical. Thing-Experience (Objectification) as De-vivification

Is there a way of avoiding these difficulties and arriving at a new solution of the problem? The common point of departure of both theories is sense data, whose explanation decides everything. Let us inquire more fundamentally: what is to be achieved by this explanation? The justification of naive consciousness and its elevation to the scientific and critical level. For this purpose one isolates whatever is discoverable in its purity as a genuine datum, whatever does not arise from the subject, whatever is not creatively produced by the psychic process, whatever has its provenance in, i.e. is caused by the external world, [85] which in this way testifies to its reality.

The naive consciousness, which includes all environmental experience, instead of deliberating upon what is immediately and primarily given, already assumes too much and makes far too many presuppositions. *What is immediately given!* Every word here is significant. What does 'immediate' mean? The lectern is given to me immediately in the lived experience of it. I see it as such, I do not see sensations and sense data. I am not conscious of sensations at all. Yet I still see brown, the brown colour. But I do not see it as a sensation of brown, as a moment of my psychic processes. I see something brown, but in a unified context of signification in connection with the lectern. But I can still disregard everything that belongs to the lectern, I can brush away everything until I arrive at the simple sensation of brown, and I can make this itself into an object. It then shows itself as something primarily given.

It is indisputable that I can do this. Only I ask myself: what does 'given' mean here? Do I experience this datum 'brown' as a moment of sensation in the same way as I do the lectern? Does it 'world' in the brown as such, apprehended as a datum? Does my historical 'I' resonate in this apprehension? Evidently not. And what does *immediately* given mean? To be sure, I do not need to derive it subsequently like an extraworldly cause; the sensation is itself there, but only in so far as I destroy what environmentally surrounds it, in so far as I remove, bracket and disregard my historical 'I' and simply practise theory, in so far as I remain primarily *in* the theoretical attitude. This primary character is only what it is when I practise theory, when the theoretical attitude is in effect, which itself is possible only as a destruction of the environmental experience.

This datum is conceived as a psychic datum which is caused, as an object, albeit one which does not belong to the external world but is within me. Where within? *In* my consciousness? [86] Is this something spatial? But the external world is spatial, the realist will answer, and it is my scientific task to investigate the way in which something psychical can know the space of the external world, the way in which the sensations of various sense organs work together, from external causes, to bring about a perception of space. But presupposing that realism could solve all these (to some degree paradoxically posed) problems, would that in any way amount to an explanation and justification of environmental experience, even if only a moment out of it were 'explained'? Let us illustrate this from the moment of spatial perception, an environmental perception. In the course of a hike through the woods I come for the first time to Freiburg and ask, upon entering the city, 'Which is the shortest way to the cathedral?' This spatial orientation has nothing to do with geometrical orientation as such. The distance to the cathedral is not a quantitative interval; proximity and distance are not a 'how much'; the most convenient and shortest way is also not something quantitative, not merely extension as such. Analogue to the time-phenomenon.

In other words: these meaningful phenomena of environmental experience cannot be explained by destroying their essential character, by denying their real meaning in order to advance a theory. Explanation through dismemberment, i.e. destruction: one wants to explain some-thing which one no longer has as such, which one cannot and will not recognize as such in its validity. And what kind of remarkable reality is this, which must first of all be explained through such bold theories?

When I attempt to explain the environing world theoretically, it collapses upon itself. It does not signify an intensification of experience, or any superior knowledge of the environment, when I attempt its dissolution and subject it to totally unclarified theories and explanations.

The incoherence of critical realism consists not just in its cancellation of the meaningful dimension of the environing world, [87] in the fact that it does not and cannot see this dimension. Instead, it already comes armed with the theory and attempts to explain one being by another. The more critical it becomes, the more incoherent it is. (There will be no further discussion here of the total helplessness of critical realism *vis-à-vis* the phenomenon of 'alien perception'.)

But critical idealism misses the problem too, if it does not also deform it, if its equating of natural reality (in the sense of the objectivity of the natural sciences) with reality as such is not also a deformation. What realism *cannot* see, idealism does not *want* to see, because it holds *stubbornly* to a *one-sided* goal. Critical idealism rests upon an unjustified absolutization of the theoretical. Sensation is for it only the X of an equation, and gets its very meaning only in the context of theoretical objectification, and *through* this objectification. Objective idealism also does not see through its blatant theory to the environing world and environmental experience. Both these directions are subject to the dominating influence of natural science.

What does it mean that both solutions hold to the fact of natural science? It is not just naturalism, as some have opined (Husserl's 'Logos' essay), but rather the general prevalence of the *theoretical*, which deforms the true problematic. It is the primacy of the theoretical. In its very *approach to the problem*, with the isolation of sense data as the elements to be explained or eliminated as unclear residues alien to consciousness, the all-determining *step into the theoretical* has already been taken. Or rather, if we observe closely, this is not a first step into the theoretical, for one is in the theoretical always and already. This is taken as self-evident, especially when one wants to pursue science and *theory* of knowledge.

[88] *What is the theoretical and what can it accomplish?* The problem of reality and objectivity leads to this basic question.

It would not be reasonable to expect an immediate solution to a problem that has hardly been seen and where the primary elements of its founding have not yet been discovered. The only person who was troubled by the problem, Emil Lask, has fallen for the Fatherland. But to find the genuine problem in him is all the more difficult because he too wished to solve it in a theoretical way. So it came about that his real accomplishments were not understood and became lost in side-issues. Where, moreover, as occurs not infrequently today, one talks about irrationalism, one theorizes in the worst way possible. We too shall not presume to broach the problem of the essence and meaningful genesis of the theoretical even in its basic lines.

It is a matter, instead, of *making the problem visible* within the scope of our previous problematic.

Let us turn back to environmental experience and widen our perspective. We can see, at least in a provisional way, that we frequently, indeed for the most part, live environmentally and experience in this way. However, a deeply ingrained obsession with the theoretical greatly hinders a genuine survey of the prevalent domain of environmental experience. The environmental experience is no spurious contingency, but lies in the essence of life in and for itself; by contrast, we become theoretically oriented only in exceptional cases. But let us stay with the lived experience of the lectern, bearing in mind that this is in no way artificial or far-fetched. Let us enter once again into its vitality. *How do I live and experience the environmental? How* is it 'given' to me? No, for something environmental to be *given* is already a theoretical infringement. It is already forcibly removed from me, from my historical 'I' ; the 'it worlds' is already no longer primary. 'Given' already signifies an inconspicuous but genuine [89] theoretical reflection inflicted upon the environment. Thus 'givenness' is already quite probably a theoretical form, and precisely for this reason it cannot be taken as the essence of the immediate environing world as environmental. Such an opinion has the single advantage of highlighting and bringing to sharp expression the unjustified supremacy of the theoretical within this essentially a-theoretical sphere, that is, in so far as it forces into theoretical form what is fundamentally foreign to theory, 'elevating' the environmental into the theoretical.

'Givenness' signifies the initial objectifying infringement of the environment, its initial placement before the *still* historical 'I'. If the authentic meaning of the environmental is in its signifying character taken out, then as something given it gets diluted to a mere thing with thingly qualities such as colour, hardness, spatiality, extension, weight, etc. Space is thing-space, time is thing-time. This process of progressively destructive theoretical infection of the environmental can be exactly followed at the phenomenal level, e.g. the series lectern, box, brown colour, wood, thing.

The question 'What kind of thing is *that*?' is directed towards the still hidden character of the environing world; the environmental attitude already lies within it. Thingliness marks out a quite original sphere distilled out of the environmental; in this sphere, the 'it worlds' has already been extinguished. The thing is merely there as such, i.e. it is real, it exists. Reality is therefore not an environmental characteristic, but lies in the essence of thingliness. It is a specifically theoretical characteristic. The meaningful is de-interpreted into this residue of being real. Experience of the environment is de-vivified into the residue of recognizing something as real. The historical 'I' is de-historicized into the residue of a specific 'I-ness' as the correlate of thingliness; and only in following through the theoretical does it have its 'who', i.e. merely 'deducible'?! [90] Phenomenologically disclosed!! Thing-experience [*Dingerfahrung*] is certainly a lived experience [*Erlebnis*], but understood *vis-à-vis* its origin from the environmental experience it is already de-vivification [*Ent-lebnis*]. There are *levels of vitality* of experience, which have nothing to do with individual chance 'life-intensity', but which are on the contrary prefigured in the essence of modes of life-experience and their worlds, i.e. in the unity of genuine life itself.

In following the motivations of this process of de-vivification one obtains the essence of the *theoretical form* (itself only a name for rich and complex interconnections, an *abbreviation*!) of objectivity. The sphere of thingliness is the lowest level of what we call the objectivity of nature. As a sphere of theoretical objectivity it is structured by a definite architectonic, a multiplicity of forms of thingliness, which have their categorial unity meaningfully prescribed from the idea of the thing. The articulation of the categories is governed by the motivational laws of 'thingliness', but the latter is not at all the 'highest genus' under which the individual categories stand.

For its part the sphere of thingliness contains certain motives for intensifying the process of theoretization. The de-interpretation of the secondary sense qualities (colours, sounds) in the physical invariants of ether- and light-waves has the theoretical sense of interpreting away

[*Ver-deutlichung*]; from the perspective of the de-vivification process it is already a highly complex level of natural-scientific objectification. The sense of reality is here also maintained. Physics does not simply become mathematics. The mass constants in physics, the specific weights, etc., are rudiments from the reality of thingliness.

Research into the various levels of theoretization and into their motivational contextures is an important concern of philosophy. In some areas lasting results are achieved, above all by the [91] Marburg school and especially by Lotze in his metaphysics (ontology; Being = to stand in relation).

But the ultimate problems remain concealed when theoretization itself is absolutized without understanding its origin in 'life', i.e. without comprehending the process of ever intensifying objectification as a process of de-vivification. One of the most difficult problems is that of *transgressing the limits of environmental experience towards initial objectification*. This, and the *problem of the theoretical as such*, can only be solved by an understanding of environmental experience and its deeper problematic.

You will also now see how deceptive it is to say that sense data are 'first' and 'immediately' given. For in this 'first' there is a veritable knot of presuppositions concerning the problem of reality and in its purportedly 'primordial' character. We saw that 'reality' has its meaning in the sphere of thingliness, itself already a theoretical sphere separated out from the environment. 'In accordance with the logical meaning of the existential judgement, that something exists means that it is determined in every aspect, determined in such a way that nothing remains indeterminate.'[2]

The question 'Is this lectern (as I experience it environmentally) real?' is therefore a *nonsensical* question. A theoretical question about the existence of my environing world – and bored into it, so to speak – distorts the meaning of this world. That which does not 'world' [*Was nicht weltet*] can certainly, and precisely on that account, exist and be real. Thus the following basic statement of essence: all that is real can 'world', but not all that 'worlds' need be real. To inquire into the reality of the environmental, in relation to which all reality already presents a repeatedly transformed and de-interpreted derivation, means to stand every genuine problematic on its head. The environmental has its genuine self-demonstration in itself.

[92] The genuine solution to the problem of the reality of the external world consists in the insight that this is no problem at all, but rather an absurdity. Critical realism as realism falls victim to this absurdity, which is

exacerbated by the desire to be 'critical'. The deeper critical realism digs, the deeper it buries itself. The incoherence of genuine objective idealism (not that of its schoolmasters and later descendants) is a difficult problem: it consists in the absolutization of the theoretical as such. Objective idealism is valuable to the degree that it poses a genuine problem.

Absurd as is the question concerning the reality of the external world, the problem of the *motivation of the sense of reality (as theoretical moment of sense) from life and first of all from environmental experience* is necessary and meaningful. Now the dogged critical realist, who for all his hefty criticism does not see any genuine problems – a standpoint that elevates the philosophical lack of problem to the status of a principle – will reply that the problem is only pushed back and resurfaces within environmental experience. *Environmental experience for its part itself presupposes reality.* The critical realist will seize upon the environment, which hitherto his realism was unable to recognize, and will also deform this with theories, through his scientific ambition to remain critical at all costs and not fall under the suspicion of dogmatism. Wherever he encounters such a presupposition, he will ruthlessly run it down and demonstrate its absurdity – thus further amplifying the already existing absurdity of naive realism. But the paradox is that genuine naivety can be achieved only through the most intimate philosophical intuition!!

How is this objection, which shifts the problem of reality precisely into the environmental sphere, to be answered? We do not answer it at all, for this objection only exponentially intensifies the absurdity.

[93] And yet it appears that we also cannot rid ourselves of the repeated objection that in environmental experience the reality of the external world is *presupposed*. But as long as we listen to this objection and take it seriously, we have not yet properly understood and overcome its absurdity.

What does it mean to say that environmental experience *presupposes* reality? It means two things: environmental experience itself presupposes, albeit 'unconsciously', the reality of the environment; and environmental experience is, from the point of view of epistemology and without further examination, *itself a presupposition*.

What does 'presuppose' mean? In what context and from what perspective does presupposing have a meaning? What does 'pre-' mean here? Obviously its intended meaning is neither spatial nor temporal. *The 'pre-' has something to do with ordering*, a 'pre-' within an order of positions, laws and posits. This does not need to be spatial, as with the number series, for example, where '2' comes before '3'. I can think '3' without 'previously' having thought '2', yet in the '3' I still presuppose the '2'. The '3' is only meaningful as determined through the '2' (however, not fully determined by this). In an analogous way a conclusion presupposes its premises. Making a presupposition means positing a proposition as valid. It does not matter whether this validity is proven or unproven, but if I posit it another proposition is also valid. So the 'pre-' refers to a relation of logical ordering, a *relation* that holds between theoretical propositions, a relation of founding and logical ground-laying: *if* this is valid, *so is that*. Instead of this hypothetical grounding, a *categorical* grounding is also possible: a '*so it is*'.

Now is it the case that in environmental experience reality is 'presupposed', even if 'unconsciously'? We saw that in environmental experience there is [94] *no theoretical positing* at all. The 'it worlds' is not established theoretically, but is experienced as 'worlding'.

But this is, viewed epistemologically, a 'presupposition', and indeed an unproven one. However, if it is not in its nature a theoretical posit, then still less is it a 'presupposition'. (If not at all a posit, then also prior to all provability and unprovability. Epistemology knows only posits, and sees everything as posit and pre-sup*posit*ion.) As such it does not let itself be seen, and when epistemology thus sees and so 'posits' environmental experience, then it destroys it in its meaning and takes it as such (as something destroyed) into a theoretical context. It sees theorized reality as *the* reality and in this way tries to explain environmental 'reality'. Only when I move in the sphere of posits can the talk of presuppositions have any meaning. *Environmental experience itself neither makes presuppositions, nor does it let itself be labelled as a presupposition. It is not even presuppositionless*, for presupposition and presuppositionlessness have any meaning only in the theoretical. If the theoretical as such becomes problematic, so also does ambiguous talk of presupposition and presuppositionlessness. These belong rather in the *most constructive* sphere of the theory of objects, a sphere that is the most derivative branch of the genealogy of meaning.

CHAPTER THREE

Primordial Science as Pre-Theoretical Science [95]

§ 18. The Circularity of Epistemology

It will be recalled that the problem of presuppositions played a major role in our introductory considerations, providing the basic impetus for putting into motion and pursuing our own problematic. The self-presupposition of primordial science (the circularity implicit in its idea) was even described as essential to philosophy and as the index of potential and genuine philosophical problems. It was also admitted that, as yet, we are not able to escape methodologically from this circularity. On the other hand there is the declaration that philosophy must intrinsically possess the aptitude for the 'supersession' [*Aufhebung*] of this apparently irremovable circularity.

At this point it becomes clear that 'circularity' itself is also a kind of positing and presupposing, albeit of a very distinctive kind. Precisely that which first is to be *posited* must be *pre*-supposed. Circularity is an eminently theoretical phenomenon, it is really the most refined expression of a purely theoretical difficulty. The methodological sense of all our previous efforts was to arrive at the limit of presuppositionlessness, i.e. at the 'primal leap' [*Ur-sprung*] or origin, and to clear away everything that is laden with presuppositions. In this way we persisted in the theoretical. Circularity is a theoretical and a *theoretically made* difficulty.

But do we obtain anything new with this insight into the theoretical character of circularity? After all, at an earlier stage we already described [96] circularity as fundamental to primordial science, and every science is as such theoretical (and not, for example, practical). But previously we did not see circularity *as* an essentially theoretical phenomenon arising through a process of de-vivification from environmental experience. We now see also that the sphere in which there is circularity, precisely because it is *theoretical, de-vivified, and thus derivative, cannot be the sphere of primordiality.*

We see this only because we are ourselves doing epistemology, thus again only at the expense of the presupposition of the idea of epistemology. The absurdity of the fundamental epistemological problem of the external world's reality, together with the genuine problem of 'reality' and of theoretical knowledge as such, can be demonstrated only by epistemological means. In this way we come back to the presupposition expressly made when we took up the problem of reality.

Can we now truly master this circularity? Can the problem of *theoretical* knowledge be solved by a *theory* of knowledge, *theory solved by theory*? As a matter of fact, logic has also been described as the theory of theory. Is there such a thing? What if this were a deception? But it must be possible, for otherwise there would be no science of knowledge and of its axioms, no fundamental science of philosophy, no primordial science at all. The circularity cannot be removed as long as primordial science is *theoretical*. Knowledge cannot get outside of itself.

If the circle is to be superseded, then there must be a science that is pre-theoretical or supra-theoretical, at any rate non-theoretical, a genuinely *primordial* science from which the theoretical itself originates. This science of the origin is such that not only does it not [97] *need* to make *presuppositions*, but, because it is not theory, it *cannot* make them: it is *prior* to or *beyond* the sphere where talk of presuppositions makes sense. *This* sense is strictly derivative, 'springing' as it does from the original spring of the origin. The complex of *theoretical* positings and value-judgements, with which we have become acquainted under the name 'teleological method', falls out completely from the sphere of primordial science. This means that every value-theory and value-*system*, indeed the very idea of a *system* that would essentially absolutize the theoretical, is illusory. So, in one of the most difficult confrontations, we stand on the front against Hegel.

For the time being, however, it is an idle undertaking to think out implications without having previously come to a clear decision. Such a decision is not reached by ambitious general programmes and outlines of systems, but only by faithful investigation of genuine individual problems, which, however, are far from being 'special problems' – such things do not exist in philosophy.

Our question is whether, in solving the problem of the environing world, of the theoretical in general, and of pre-suppositions, epistemology is not already presupposed. For even if we show that there is no genuine epistemological problem, we must still do epistemology. The answer depends on whether there really is anything at all like epistemology, theory of the theoretical, theory of theory. How is this to be clarified?

§ 19. How to Consider Environmental Experience

The question cannot be decided by dialectical exercises, but by attempting to understand how we gained *insight* into the absurdity of the customary problem of reality. [98] We are concerned here not with presumptions and playful paradoxes but with genuine insights. How were these obtained? The basic problem is clear, namely the problem of the method-ological apprehension of lived experiences as such: how is a science of experiences as such possible? We wish to decide this question by looking at how environmental experience is to be considered.

Although we are still very much at the preliminary stage of phenomen-ological method, it is now already necessary to clarify the basic feature of our fundamental methodological attitude. We shall therefore enact the environmental experience in its full vitality, in order not only to look at it, but to look at this look and at *how* the first look is enacted. The absolute-ness of seeing cannot be attained all at once, in artificial and manipulative fashion, but in the first instance only by radically excluding all relativities (which are essentially theoretical prejudices).

We have seen that environmental experience does not involve any-thing like a substantive positing of things, nor even a consciousness of givenness. We further discovered that experiential comportment does not concentrate and terminate in an objectification, that the environing world does not stand there with a fixed index of existence, but floats away in the experiencing, bearing within it the rhythm of experience, and can be experienced only in this rhythmic way. But in the bare experience of a thing there is a peculiar breach between experiencing and experienc*ed*: the latter has broken out of the rhythm that characterized the minimal experience and stands for itself, intended only in knowledge. The sphere of objects is characterized by merely being intended, such that knowledge *aims* at this sphere. The sense of reality is the intendability of all that is thinglike as persevering in a multiplicity of experiences.

a) The Method of Descriptive Reflection (Paul Natorp) [99]

We have 'looked', therefore, at two experiences. But let us be clear about what, in both cases, we did not see. We did not see anything psychic, i.e. we saw no object sphere that was merely intended, and indeed intended as a qualitatively specific region of the psychical different from the physical. The opposition between the psychical and the physical did not enter our field of view at all, nor did any thing-like occurrences, any processes.

However, we did see something, namely life-experiences. We are no longer living in the experiences, but looking at them. The lived experiences now become looked-at experiences. 'Only through reflectively *experiencing* [*erfahrende*] acts do we *know* something of the stream of living experience.'[1] Through reflection [*Reflexion*] every living experience can be turned into something looked at. 'The phenomenological method operates entirely in acts of reflection.'[2] Reflections are themselves in turn lived experiences and as such can in turn be reflectively considered, 'and so on *ad infinitum*, as a universal principle'.[3]

Let us make these connections completely clear. Let us place ourselves within a thing-experience (not in an environmental experience, which involves more difficult connections). We are describing a thing as given in an objective manner: it is coloured, extended, etc. Living within this description, the view of the 'consciousness-I' [*Bewußtseins-Ich*] is directed at the thing (like a searchlight). Now the ray of consciousness can itself be directed at the describing comportment, as if a searchlight's ray searches out itself, seeking its first ray. But the image is misleading, for [100] only another searchlight could do this, whereas it is really the same 'I' that reflects upon itself. Unlike the searchlight case, this same 'I' directs itself not towards something objective, but towards a life-experience, towards what is of the same essence as reflection. Reflection itself belongs to the sphere of life-experience as one of its 'fundamental peculiarities'. The field of experience provided in reflection, the stream of experience, becomes *describable*. The science of experiences is a descriptive one. Every descriptive science 'has its justification in itself'.[4] The experiences of perception, of memory, of representation, of judgement, of I, you and us (types of experience of persons) can thus be described. Experiences are not explained psychologically, nor referred back to physiological processes and psychic dispositions. No hypotheses are made about them, but we simply bring out what lies in the experiences themselves (in the way we did in the two experiences already described).

Is this method of descriptive reflection (or reflective description) capable of investigating the sphere of experience and disclosing it scientifically? The reflection makes something which was previously unexamined, something merely unreflectively experienced, into something '*looked at*'. We look at it. In reflection it stands before us as an object of reflection, we are directed towards it and make it into an object as such, standing over against us. Thus, in reflection we are theoretically orientated. All theoretical comportment, we said, is de-vivifying. This now shows itself in the case of life-experiences, for in reflection they are no longer lived but looked at. We set the experiences *out* before us *out of* immediate experience; we intrude so to speak into the flowing stream of experiences and pull one or more of them out, we [101] 'still the stream' as Natorp says.[5] (Until now Natorp is the only person to have brought scientifically noteworthy objections against phenomenology. Husserl himself has not yet commented on these.)

The stilled stream of lived experiences now becomes a series of individually intended objects. 'Reflection necessarily has an analytical, so to speak dissective or chemically destructive effect upon what is experienced.'[6] For any kind of cognitive seizure of experience to be possible, a theoretical orientation is inevitable. Theoretical experiences themselves are only theoretically apprehensible. Epistemology is nothing but theoretical forming and shaping.

Phenomenology's claim to be purely descriptive in its intent changes nothing in regard to its theoretical character. For description also already proceeds via concepts: it is a *circumscription* of something into generalities, it is 'subsumption' (Natorp); it already presupposes a certain kind of concept-formation and therefore 'abstraction' (Natorp) and theory, i.e. 'mediation' (Natorp). Description is nothing immediate and unmediated, but has a necessary relation to knowledge of laws. Description is unthinkable without underlying explanation. Description as knowledge of facts is already objectifying, and only as such, in so far as it is 'propaedeutic' to the knowledge of laws (explanation),[7] does it possess any value. It is 'in all circumstances a grasping-in-words . . . all verbal expression is generalizing, a moulding from and for generalities. The concept is the logical vehicle of generality.'[8] If one wishes to make experience into an object of science, it is impossible to avoid theoretization. This means, however, that there is no immediate apprehension of experience.

[102] In the following I shall attempt – without any detailed consideration of Natorp – further to develop the problems on the basis of

phenomenology. Since Natorp's critique and his own positive conceptions are so difficult, and above all since they have grown out of the Marburg school's fundamental position, I will not venture an extensive discussion of them here. Our problem of the theoretical has emerged from deeper contexts, and we have already seen that critical idealism does not see these. The whole scientific type of the Marburgers has therefore permeated our problem, so that precisely for this reason I can allow Natorpian objections to come up, because they themselves stem from the theoretical standpoint. Only the general direction of Natorp's solution – and so far he has given nothing more than this – will be indicated.

Accordingly, Natorp says that there can be only a *mediated* apprehension of experiences, and that working out the method of this mediate apprehension, of genuine subjectification (the 'objectification' of the subjective), is one of the most difficult problems. Phenomenology, with its view that consciousness, life-experiences, can be absolutely given, confuses a requirement with its only possible mode of fulfilment.[9] What is *required*, as the aim of knowledge, is the 'absolute' presentation of experiences, analogous to that of *objects*. This does not mean, however, that they are 'absolutely' attainable, immediately, but only in and through mediation (double-meaning of 'absolute'). All objectification is accomplished by the consciousness, i.e. by the 'subjective'. In this way Natorp already gives the problem a definite turn. Objectification is determination, the subjective is what determines; it is prior, 'this side of all determination'.[10] *Is it also prior to all possible determinablility?*

b) Reconstruction as the Characteristic Moment of the Method. Subjectification and Objectification [103]

How can that which is itself essentially determining be in turn determinable? Self-observation is normally called reflection (reflector: mirror). Through reflective analysis experiences are disturbed, reshaped, distorted. What if this disturbing distortion could be reversed? If a method of reversal were possible, if a means of extinguishing the destructive influence of analysis were available, would this not amount to genuine, albeit mediated, knowledge of the immediate?

As a matter of fact Natorp holds that such a means is 'in a certain way possible'. Through this new method the complexion of the subjective, which analysis had dissected into its individual component parts, is determinable 'as it was given prior to analysis'.[11] Indeed the more consciously analysis progresses, so to speak, boring into and dissecting the complexion, the more do the specific elements emerge, and the greater becomes the multiplicity of possible reciprocal relations among them. Ever richer lines of connection can course between these points of relation, with ever increasing differentiation being added to what has previously been developed, the interpretation itself becoming more unified and determinate, more contained and complete. 'From the original life of consciousness', more and more can be 'theoretically regained'.[12] The finitude of the destroyed complexion is brought back to the infinity of their reciprocity, the *discretion* of points brought to the *continuum* of its lines of connections. 'Point-by-point thinking, *discretion*, and thinking of the totality, the totality of the series, by means of universality, universality of points, [104] *continuity*, these two are one, the "synthetic" unity.'[13]

A characteristic moment of this new method now becomes visible. The analysis is not an end in itself, not a goal but only a *means*, a transitional stage to the real aim of 'concretization'. The result of this is the highest attainable (having undergone the analysis) determinateness. What was previously destroyed is now restored, the whole complexion is '*reconstructed*'.

The scientific method of conceiving consciousness, of apprehending the subjective, the genuine method of philosophical psychology, is 'reconstruction'. This method of subjectification, as can easily be seen, is not *prior* to the method of objectification but *subsequent* to it.

Already for primitive, natural consciousness, what is first of all given are objects, and indeed objects of knowledge. Reflection [*Besinnung*] comes relatively late to the givenness of the *knowledge* of objects. The sphere of appearance, in and through which objects are constituted, for a long time lies hidden on this side of all objectively oriented consideration. Such consideration, scientific knowledge in its true form, proceeds in a thoroughly 'constructive' fashion.[14] Such construction arrives at the scientific 'concepts' that determine objectivity. Science provides experience of its objects by way of objectification. Now the clearer the individual stages and steps taken by scientific knowledge in creating this objectivity, the more consciously objectification presents itself in its structure and in this consciousness becomes fulfilled, the easier and more sure becomes the subsequent counter-movement of reconstructing the appearance [105] from which, through steps of objectification, objectivity was created.

Even ordinary representations and pre-scientific knowledge are already 'objectifications', 'albeit mostly of less rigorous and secure contours'[15] of conceptuality; they differ only in degrees from genuine scientific object-ification. The aesthetic, ethical and religious consciousness are also objectifications; they lay claim to objective lawfulness. Particularly at the level of higher cultures they strive for the ideal of universally valid objectivity, an ideal that persists even if it is not yet reached. The highest degree of consciousness and the most complete analysis of the steps of objectification are achieved in philosophy, more precisely in the philosophical sciences of objectivity: logic, ethics, aesthetics, philosophy of religion. From this objectified structure and its analytically presented steps or stations, *the subjective foundation is to be attained through reverse argumentation*.[16] Philosophical psychology is therefore not the *foundation* for logic, ethics . . . but rather their *conclusion* and scientific completion.

Two things must be held clearly in view: first the *exact correspondence* of the two tasks of objectification and subjectification; second the *ground-laying* character of *objectification for* subjectification. In other words, nothing can be reconstructed that was not previously constructed.[17] Objectification and subjectification signify nothing but two different directions of the path of knowledge: from appearance to object, and from object to appearance. They are not different heterogeneous regions of facts within consciousness, but only two different senses of direction, the plus and the minus sense of knowledge: [106] 'Something, an object, appears to me and I am conscious of it, which is substantively one thing and not two.'[18] It is just the double-direction of the unitary path of knowledge. In the unity of consciousness there is constituted, through the unity of its lawfulness, the unity of the multiplicity of objectivity. The fundamental relation between law, object and consciousness is the *fundamental equation of consciousness*, already brought to sharpest expression by Kant, and found by Natorp already in Plato's 'idea' and its function συλλαβεῖν εἰς ἕν [to comprehend into a unity].[19] The process of objectification has its infinitely distant goal in the unity of objectivity, the unity of the lawfulness of consciousness. And precisely the law of this lawfulness is the infinite aim of the opposite road of knowledge, that of subjectification. The two meet up and become identical in the infinite. 'The problem of the concrete is nothing else but that of the (intensive) infinite . . . The *a posteriori* must be *produced* from the *a priori* in the same way that individual links in the series are determined through their law, solely in relation to the whole series, through which they *are* what they are.'[20] 'To a givenness there must correspond an active *giving*.'[21] This has an analogue 'in mathematics where the "infinitely distant point" is not double, but is one and the same for proceeding in the plus and in the minus direction of one and the same straight line'.[22] What is absolute is basically just the lawfulness of the method of objectification and subjectification, the two directions *of* knowledge.[23]

c) Critique of Natorp's Method [107]

A comprehensive critical treatment of this method would require a deeper penetration into the problems than we have so far achieved. Our critical question must be restricted to the domain of our problem, namely the scientific disclosure of the sphere of lived experience.

Does and can the method of reconstruction achieve what it is supposed to? *No*, for first of all it too is objectification. Natorp in no way shows that his *method* is different from that of objectification. For reconstruction is also construction (mathematical discreteness and mathematical continuity are basically one), and it is precisely characteristic of objectification to be constructive, thus theoretical. Above all there is no way of seeing how the unmediated immediate is supposed to be attainable at all through a mediated theoretization along the path of dissective analysis. From where is the standard for reconstruction to be obtained? Natorp denies that the immediate can be given prior to all analysis. How can reconstruction determine the complexion 'as it was given prior to analysis'?[24] And supposing that it were determined, then, since all determination is logical, it would again be objectified. Natorp is himself quite clear about this, for 'psycho*logy* is in a sense logicization, namely ultimate logical *grounding* of the psychic'.[25] There is no danger of logic becoming psychology, but rather genuine psycho*logy* becomes logic. This conforms to Natorp's ultimate idea of the unified philosophical system as the utmost 'inevitable universalization of the transcendental problem': the logic 'of the object-relation [108] in general, from which all these [logical, ethical, aesthetic, religious] particular directions of knowledge, of object-positing, must proceed as necessary emanations'.[26] The most radical absolutization of the theoretical and logical, an absolutization that has not been proclaimed since Hegel. (Unmistakable connections with Hegel: everything unmediated is mediated.) An absolutization that radically logicizes the sphere of experience and lets this exist only in the logicized form of the concretion of the *concrete* – which concrete has meaning only in its necessary correlation with the abstract, whereby, however, the logical is not left behind.

With this problem of the ultimate systematic universalization of the logical Natorp believes himself to be in agreement with the main directions of philosophy. (Husserl's idea of formal ontology and logic as *mathesis universalis* – Leibniz – has an unmistakable affinity with Natorp's universal logic of objects. But it does not have this systematic representation in the way Natorp sees things.)

With this absolutization of the logical Natorp can see the representation of things only as a rudimentary preliminary stage of genuine logical positing of objects (in science). If he were to acknowledge an original sphere of lived experience such as the environmental, it could only be as *crude* objectification.

Natorp's systematic pan-logical fundamental orientation blocks him from any free access to the sphere of lived experience, to consciousness. For him this remains essentially a theoretical consciousness of objects, resolved into the lawfulness of constitution (cf. typically: the fundamental equation of consciousness).

The insight into the non-primordiality of the theoretical comportment shows that Natorp, for all his acumen, [109] has not exhausted all possibilities. His exclusively theoretical attitude, i.e. his absolutization of logic, also cannot exhaust them. His dispute with phenomenology does not get at its authentic sphere of problems at all.

This applies quite generally to all previous criticisms of phenomenology. Their purported force derives from a preconceived position, whether this be the standpoint of transcendental philosophy, empirical psychology, or post-Hegelianism. The fundamental *demand of phenomenology to bracket all standpoints is everywhere overlooked*. This is decisive proof that the authentic sense of phenomenology is not understood. When the proper fundamental attitude to phenomenology is lacking, all objections to it, however sophisticated and significant they might be, are fallacious.

§ 20. Phenomenological Disclosure of the Sphere of Lived Experience

The fundamental methodological problem of phenomenology, the question concerning the scientific disclosure of the sphere of lived experience, itself stands under phenomenology's 'principle of principles'. Husserl formulates it thus: '*Everything* that presents itself . . . *originarily in "intuition"* is to be taken simply . . . as it gives itself.'[27] This is the 'principle of principles', in regard to which 'no conceivable theory can lead us astray'.[28] If by a principle one were to understand a theoretical proposition, this designation would not be fitting. However, that Husserl speaks of a *principle* of principles, of something that precedes all principles, in regard to which no theory can lead us astray, already shows (although Husserl does not explicitly say so) that it does not have a theoretical character. [110] It is the primordial intention of genuine life, the primordial bearing of life-experience and life as such, the absolute *sympathy with life* that is identical with life-experience. To begin with, i.e. coming along this path from the theoretical while freeing ourselves more and more from it, we always *see* this basic bearing, we have an orientation *to* it. The same basic bearing first becomes absolute when we live in it – and that is not achieved by any constructed system of concepts, regardless of how extensive it may be, but only through phenomenological life in its ever-growing self-intensification.

All this is separated by a chasm from every kind of *logicism*, and has not the slightest connection with the *philosophy of feeling* or with inspired philosophizing. This primal habitus of the phenomenologist cannot be appropriated overnight, like putting on a uniform, and it will lead to formalism and concealment of all genuine problems if this habitus is treated merely mechanically in the manner of a routine.

The *'rigour'* of the scientificity awakened in phenomenology gains its original sense from this basic bearing and is incomparable with the 'rigour' of derivative non-primordial sciences. At the same time it becomes clear why the problem of method is more central in phenomenology than in any other science. (For this reason, this whole lecture-course has actually pivoted around the problem of method.)

For our problem, the basic bearing of phenomenology yields a decisive directive: not to construct a method from outside or from above, not to contrive a new theoretical path by exercises in dialectic. Since phenomenology can prove itself only through itself, every taking-up of a standpoint is a sin against its ownmost spirit. And the *original sin* would be the opinion that *it is itself a standpoint*.

a) Objections to Phenomenological Research [111]

The problem of method presented itself in the form of the question of the possible description of experiences. The crudest, but already sufficiently threatening objection, pertained to *language*. All description is a 'grasping-in-words' – 'verbal expression' is generalizing. This objection rests on the opinion that all language is itself already objectifying, i.e. that living in meaning implies a theoretical grasping of what is meant, that the fulfilment of meaning is without further ado *only* object-giving [*gegenstandgebend*].

Along with this undemonstrated prejudice the opinion is advanced that the generalization of the meaning function, its character of universality, is identical with the theoretical and conceptual universality of the genus concept, i.e. that there is only the theoretical universality of a genus and that all verbal meaning consists in nothing but this, that all meaning is in itself already '*opining*' [*meinend*].

But the theoretical prejudices go still deeper: phenomenological seeing (whose essence we have not exposed with greater precision) is simply identified with description. It is not yet settled that seeing, the intuition out of which a description first arises, has a totally different character. If description itself is always necessarily theoretization, that does not exclude the possibility that the founding intuition – I must first see before I describe – would not be of a theoretical nature. And there always remains the problem of the formulability of what is seen. But let us go further: is phenomenological intuition a seeing to which the thing to be seen stands opposed, over against and (so to speak) outside this seeing? In other words, is this not already a disguised theory which stamps the sphere of experience as something given which is then to be described? Is there really [112] this division and separation between knowledge and object, between the given (giveable) and the description? Are we not succumbing here to a deception of language, and in fact a theoreticized language?

But if phenomenological research is a 'comportment towards something', then this involves an unavoidable objectification, an absolutely irremovable moment of theoretization. When we formulate it in this way, we are even using the highest level of theoretization, which also resides in the unities of meaning and signifying connections of language. If it is not radically to nullify itself, a meaning must in every instance mean *something*. Is Natorp in the end correct about the fundamental equation of consciousness, which brings to expression its primal theoretical character?

b) Characterization of the Levels of De-vivification. The Pre-worldly Something and the Something of Knowability

In order not to fall into confusion and so distort the phenomenological attitude from the ground up, a fundamental division must be made clear: we have at least a rough knowledge of the process of theoretization in regard to its origin and its progressive de-vivification. Up to now, the pinnacle appeared to be the utterly empty and formal character of the objectified 'something'. In this all content is extinguished, its sense lacks all relation to a world-content be it ever so radically theorized. It is the absolutely worldless, world-foreign; it is the sphere which takes one's breath away and where no one can live.

Is this characterization of the levels of de-vivification, culminating in a mere something in general, an 'anything whatsoever', at all tenable? Does it correspond to the genuine comportmental phenomena? [113] Let us again bring to mind the environmental experience: the lectern. Starting from what is here experienced I proceed to theorize: it is brown; brown is a colour; colour is a genuine sense datum; a sense datum is the result of physical or physiological processes; the primary cause is physical; this cause objectively is a determinate number of ether-waves; ether is made up of simple elements; linking these are simple laws; the elements are ultimate; *the elements are something in general.*

These judgements may be made in any kind of confused temporal order. But if we attend to their meaning, and to the connections defined by the fact that a judgement is motivated by one and only one thing out of the multiplicity, what emerges instead from the potential disorder of factual contingencies is a definitely directed gradation and hierarchical ordering. To go into the individual motives and motivators would be too difficult. Let us look rather at the conclusion of the motivational process, i.e. at the highest theoretization. Is this motivated in the leading principle 'The elements are ultimate'? Undoubtedly, deeper in its motive, right down to the environmental experience. But you surely have the inchoate feeling that something is not right here.

Do we then have to traverse all the motivating steps, beginning from the perception of brown, in order to be able ('able' according to the possibility of sense and its enactment) to judge that 'it is something'? Does not every theoreticized level of reality, in respect of the particular items of reality belonging to it, allow for the judgement, 'it is something'? And does not this ultimate theoretical characterization of the bare something in general fall out of the order entirely, such that any and every level can motivate it? This is *in fact* the case, or more precisely for what is coming – *in essence*: it can be brought to evidence that [114] at any and every level there is the possibility of intending it theoretically as a mere something. Bring this to full evidence for yourselves, but also consider whether at every level the potential motive exists for the judgement that it is brown. Or for the judgement that it is colour. Not at all! These theoretizations are restricted to a particular sphere of reality. I call it *the specific level-boundedness of the steps in the process of de-vivification*. In contrast to this the formal theoretization is evidently free. From this state of essence, new evidences immediately spring out:

1) the motivation for formal theoretization must be *qualitatively* different; accordingly
2) it does not belong in the sequence of steps of the specific levels of de-vivification; accordingly
3) formal theoretization is then also not the pinnacle, the highest point in the de-vivification process.

What previously counted as eminently theoretical, proves not at all to belong to the de-vivification process. Accordingly there would be two fundamentally different sorts of the theoretical, whose essential connection at first poses a great problem. However, conclusions in phenomenology are always dangerous, and as long as they have not been proven to be evident in their content, they are worthless.

It may well be that the formally objective does not initially have any connection at all with the theoretical process, i.e. that its motivational origin from life is qualitatively and essentially different, that therefore it is not appropriate to speak simply of *types* and differences in type regarding the processes of possible theoretization.

We said that *formal objectification is free*, i.e. that it is not bound to steps and levels. *Each* level can in itself be considered from a formal point of view. Formal characterization demands no specific motivation at a particular level within the theoretization process. [115] But it is also not simply bound to the theoretical sphere, the domain of objects as such. The range of possible formally objective characterizations is obviously greater. (I refer to what was said earlier.) The environmental is something; what is worth taking is something; the valid is something; everything worldly, be it, for example, aesthetic, religious or social in type, is something. *Anything that can be experienced at all is a possible something, irrespective of its genuine world-character.* The meaning of 'something' is just 'the experienceable as such'. The indifference of the 'anything whatsoever' in regard to every genuine world character and every particular species of object is in no way identical with de-vivification, or even with the latter's highest level, the most sublime theoretization. It does not mean an absolute interruption of the life-relation, no easing of de-vivification, no theoretical fixing and freezing of what can be experienced. It is much more the index for the highest potentiality of life. Its meaning resides in the fullness of life itself, and implies that this still has no genuine worldly characterization, but that the motivation for such quite probably is living in life. It is the *'not-yet'*, i.e. not yet broken out into genuine life, it is the essentially *pre-worldly*. But this means that the sense of the something as the experienceable implies the moment of 'out towards' [*auf zu*], of 'direction towards', *'into* a (particular) world', and indeed in its undiminished 'vital impetus'.

The 'something' as the pre-worldly as such must not be conceived theoretically, in terms of a physiological and genetic consideration. It is a basic phenomenon that can be experienced in understanding, e.g. in the living situation of gliding from one world of experience to another genuine life-world, or in moments of especially intensive life; not at all or seldom in those types of experience that are firmly anchored in a world *without* reaching, precisely within this world, a much greater life-intensity.

[116] The something as the experienceable as such is not anything radically theoreticized and de-vivified, but is to be regarded rather as a moment of essence of life in and for itself, which itself stands in a close relation with the character of the appropriating event of experiences as such. The formal objective *something of knowability* is *first* of all motivated from this pre-worldly something of life [*Lebens-etwas*]. A something of formal theoretization. The tendency into a world can be theoretically deflected *prior* to its expression. Thus the universality of the formally objective appropriates its origin from the in-itself of the flowing experience of life.

Seen *in this way*, from the pre-worldly, understood from life in and for itself, the formally objective is no longer a *re*-cept [*Rück-griff*] but already a con-cept [*Be-griff*]. Radical displacement of the comportment that understands life-experience. Later to be clarified are: *re-cept* (motivation), *pre-cept* [*Vorgriff*] (tendency), *concept* (object). Pre-cepts and re-cepts ('sight'), prospective grips and retrospective grips.

To be sharply separated therefore are: the pre-worldly something of life in itself, the formally objective arising from this (only from this?) as de-vivification, and the objectlike [*objektartig*] theoretical. The first sphere, as that of life, is absolute, the two others are relative, conditioned. They exist by the grace of an 'if' – if de-vivified, the experienceable looks like this and this, and is graspable only in concepts. This *fundamental 'if'* belongs to the object-specific and to the formally objective derived therefrom; this is, understood in terms of motivation, the common moment of the sphere of the formally objective and the sphere of the object.

c) Hermeneutical Intuition

It now becomes clear to what extent the motivation of the formally objective is qualitatively different from that of the object-specific, and how the former at once refers *back* to a fundamental level of life in and for itself. Signification therefore, [117] linguistic expression, does not need to be theoretical or even object-specific, but is primordially living and experiential, whether *pre-worldly or worldly*.

What is essential about the pre-worldly and worldly signifying functions is that they express the characters of the appropriating event, i.e. they go together (experiencing and experiencing experienced) with experience itself, they live in life itself and, going along with life, they are at once originating and carry their provenance in themselves. They are at once preceptive and retroceptive, i.e. they express life in its motivated tendency or tending motivation.

The empowering experiencing of living experience that takes itself along is the understanding intuition, the *hermeneutical intuition*, the originary phenomenological back-and-forth formation of the recepts and precepts from which all theoretical objectification, indeed every transcendent positing, falls out. Universality of word meanings primarily indicates something originary: worldliness [*Welthaftigkeit*] of experienced experiencing.

At this point the puzzling presence of determination prior to all theoretical description is clarified. Theoretically I come out of experiencing as from a provenance; something experienceable is still brought along from this experiencing, with which one does not know what to do, and for which the convenient title of the irrational has been invented.

Problem of heterothesis, negation. Motivation – motivator and motive. Life is historical; no dissection into essential elements, but connection and context. Problem of material giving is not genuine, but comes only from theory.

Phenomenology and Transcendental Philosophy of Value

Summer Semester 1919

INTRODUCTION

a) Guiding Principles of the Lecture-Course

General character of the lecture-course: not a systematic and complete summarizing description reproducing two counterposed standpoints and systems (that would result in either a poor imitation of a much better original or a worthless one-sided picture which would only add to our problems).

Aim: concrete problems, which arise from the central tendency of the problematic and cluster around a concrete fundamental problem. Judgement as acknowledging. (In general: intentionality, the tendency of lived experience, and the question of how far values can be excluded in teleologically interpreted tendencies!)

Undertaking basic investigations, which must precede all serious discussion on 'standpoints' (i.e. overcome this and expose it as superfluous).

Three groups of problems:

I value problem	system (III) of	reduction to the
II form problem[1]	teleological (I)	phenomenon of
III system problem	idealism (II)	motivation

It is first a matter of gaining definition of these problems, i.e. of tracing them back to their genuinely originary phenomenological level (*life in and for itself*). *Historical introduction*: motivation and tendency of the three problem-ideas in intellectual history.

[122] I) With the continuing retreat of speculative idealism[2] came the reactive threat of an absolute reification of spirit into things, bodies, movements and processes. Every metaphysics of Being was regarded as a relapse. At the same time one recognized, partly as an after-effect of German idealism, the impossibility of any kind of metaphysical, non-material, non-sensory orientation.

In the ought, and in value as that which is ultimately experienced, Lask discovered *the* world: something non-material [*nicht-sachlich*], non-sensorily metaphysical, but also not unmaterial [*unsachlich*], not extravagantly speculative, but rather factual.

This fundamental conviction (grounded in the ought) made possible a worldview, a harmonizing of science (natural science) and the life of the spirit; at the same time it introduced a new perspective on scientific-philosophical problems, a perspective that allows the initial renewal of Kant to be understood and to be brought to a unified interpretation as worldview (normativity – teleological method).

The development of modern philosophy of value runs in two main currents: on the one hand an ever more incisive working of the idea of value into the transcendental, on the other hand an ever more conscious transcendental formulation of problems of value. Both main currents grow out of the idea of value and as such are historically determined: 1) through the reawakened theoretical problems (Windelband's essay on the negative judgement in *Preludes*; Rickert's *Doctrine of Definition* and *Object of Knowledge*[3]); 2) through the [123] entry into philosophical consciousness of 'history' as a philosophical problem (Dilthey's decisive distinction influenced Windelband's rectoral address,[4] Rickert, Lask's 'Fichte' essay). The theoretical as value in the case of Rickert, categories as value and form in the case of Lask. Windelband, on the other hand, does not conceive the theoretical in terms of value.

II) Through the ever more precise conception of the problem of value and the effect of Marburg Neo-Kantianism and Husserl's *Logical Invest-igations*,[5] the problematic of value underwent a growing incorporation into the transcendental. This increasingly prominent character of the problem of form (Lask's *Logic and Judgement*, to be compared with the individual editions of Rickert's *Object of Knowledge*[6]), the transcendental consideration of form, leads to the problem of categorial divisions into regions. Efforts in the philosophy of history, culminating in the philosophy of culture, make obvious the necessity of a cultural whole and its possible total interpretation. Interpretation is possible only in and through the totality of cultural values; their connection and rank-order become problematic.

III) The problematics of transcendental theory and philosophy of history carry over into the *systematics*, the system of values (Lask, conclusion of *Logic*;[7] Rickert's 'Logos' article and *Limits*). The systematics itself moves into the proximity of the Hegelian heterothesis, which at the same time is seen in the theoretical sphere of objects: form/content duality. Systematics is driven by the general need at this time for a [124] philosophical system, e.g. by the awakening Neo-Hegelianism, by the desire to escape from 'fragmentation and the particular sciences' (cf. also Simmel's typical approximation of a system). To be sure, only in a systematics built from fragmentation.

The historical effect of the philosophy of value was a strong emphasis on the idea of value in all spheres of life, a broadening of the axiological by analogy to theoretization, partly also a prevalence of both in a variegated penetration.

These historical motivations of the three problem constellations allow the philosophy of value to be understood as strongly conditioned by the *nineteenth century*. The basic conviction of the primacy of value is so universal that it survives the acceptance of diverse influences and problem-directions, so that the syncretic character of philosophy of value apparently wanes.

To be sure, this would lead nowhere if the originality of this philosophy were to dissolve into nothing, assuming that it poses genuine problems and solves them by genuine means – for many still regard originality as a criterion for the significance or insignificance of a philosophy: so-called historical consideration of diverse systems, their short life-span, their character as typical forms of expression of a personality or historical period – unscientific attitudes towards history encourage such assessments. However, what is decisive is not *originality* of worldview and system, but *originality* of scientific problems. The one neither excludes nor includes the other! What is decisive is not novelty in composing problems, but primordiality of the problems themselves from their immanent meaning.

So it could happen that in respect of philosophy of value not only could originality disappear (in so far as it is only clever assumptions and cleverly exploited [125] combinations of partly genuine insights: Dilthey, Brentano), but also its originality could be proved not to exist, indeed (which alone is scientifically decisive) could turn out to be not only *factually* absent but *impossible*. We want to understand the reasons for this impossibility, i.e. for the lack of a genuine scientific problematic. This can be achieved only by concrete analysis of problems.

The *universal, methodological,* at the beginning! *Phenomenology and historical method*; their absolute unity in the purity of the understanding of life in and for itself (cf. by contrast the Marburg conception of the history of philosophy, or Hönigswald, *Ancient Philosophy*[8]).

Phenomenological-scientific confrontation with a philosophy that has already achieved its expression in intellectual history must, in order to secure real understanding, embrace two kinds of task. First it must understand the motivations in intellectual history for the historically factual expression of this type of philosophy, second it must understand this type of philosophy in the genuineness of its own problematic.

It is wrong to think that these two types of consideration are different in that one is historical, the other systematic. No genuine historical understanding can occur without returning to the original motivations, nor is such a system scientifically possible. That is, since the whole division into historical and systematic, a division that still rules philosophy everywhere today, is not a genuine one, it is possible to show positively how phenomenologico-historical discussion presents a unitary and primordial method of phenomenological research.

General considerations on philosophical critique: by its nature phenomenological critique can never be negative, that is, a [126] demonstration of contradictions, absurdities, incoherencies and fallacies. Absurdity, on the other hand, is not logical-theoretical inconsistency, one thing opposing another thing. Instead, all theorizing dialectic is contrary to the sense of the already given and giveable.

Phenomenological criterion: none of the above-mentioned predicates belongs in the domain of phenomenological criteria. A phenomenological criterion is just the understanding evidence [*die verstehende Evidenz*] and the evident understanding of experience, of life in and for itself in the *eidos*. Phenomenological critique is not refutation or counter-demonstration. Instead, the proposition to be criticized is understood from its origin, from *where* its meaning derives. Critique is a positive sounding out of genuine motivations. Motivations that are not genuine are not motivations at all, and can be understood only via the genuine ones. What is phenomenologically genuine authenticates itself and does not require a further (theoretical) criterion.

Absolute rehabituation in respect of scientific demands and expect-ations. Quality and intensity of understanding is decisive. Quantity, degree of complexity, completeness, and ordering of the paragraphs are side-issues. These do not advance the proceeding at all, but only dampen the vitality of the understanding experiences.

Transposition in the sensibility for the absoluteness of originary evidences. Immersion in the lack of need for theoretical proofs and reasons and explanations from the total system. *Restructuring and novel distribution of the duties of proof.* Not overlooking and overhearing the interlocking evidences. Everything that burdens and retards arguments with objections is not only without purpose in phenomenology, but also against its spirit.

Questioning in phenomenology is not constructive, conceptually deduct-ive and dialectical, but springs from and aims at the what, the *quale* of the phenomena; no free-floating, unfounded *conceptual questions*!

b) Aim of the Lecture-Course [127]

The unstressed and indifferent juxtaposition of phenomenology and tran-scendental philosophy of value in the title of this lecture-course brings its real intention only vaguely to expression: what we aim at, concretely put, is a *phenomenological critique* of transcendental philosophy of value.

It is, therefore, *not* simply a matter of perhaps interesting contrasts between one philosophical '*standpoint*' and another, or of playing off one 'direction' against another. Rather, every kind of standpoint-philosophy will, through the ruthless radicalism of our problematic, prove to be pseudo-philosophy, and in such a way that we press forward into the genuinely primordial level of a genuine philosophical problematic and methodology. Genuine critique is always positive – and phenomeno-logical critique especially, given that it is phenomenological, can as such *only* be positive. It overcomes and rejects confused, half-clarified false problematics only through *demonstration* of the genuine sphere of problems. It dispenses with the industrious searching-out of logical discrepancies in particular systems, with the sounding-out of so-called inner contradictions and with the refuting of isolated errors in theories.

Phenomenology is concerned with the principles of all spiritual life and insight into the essence of all that is itself principled. At the same time this means that phenomenological critique, whose positive aim is to see and bring into view the true and genuine origins of spiritual life as such, will occupy itself only with such philosophical intuitions as have the tendency, through critical phenomenological research, to lead into genuine problem fields.

[128] Such an engagement will become scientifically obligatory only in respect of a philosophy that is based on serious work and that raises the claim to scientificity, but which is also determined to advance the great traditions of Kant and German idealism in their enduring tendencies. Such an engagement concerns the nineteenth century in general. Along with the Marburg school, the transcendental philosophy of value is one of the most important philosophical currents of the present day. It is also called the Baden or Freiburg school, which was fitting before 1916, when Windelband taught in Heidelberg, and Rickert, his student and the systematic founder of philosophy of value, taught here in Freiburg.

Since for every phenomenological investigation it is of decisive importance to understand the genuine and meaningful motives of a problem, the task arises of making evident the problematic of transcendental philosophy of value in its immanent historico-intellectual motivations. This is not a tallying up and summary of so-called 'historical influences', but rather an understanding . . .[9]

PART ONE

Historical Presentation of the Problem [129]

CHAPTER ONE

The Genesis of Philosophy of Value as the Cultural Philosophy of the Present

§ 1. The Concept of Culture in the Philosophy of the Late Nineteenth Century

The nineteenth century brought its characteristic spiritual content and structure on to a conceptual level in its final decade and at the beginning of the twentieth century, i.e. it created its own typical philosophy of worldview. 'Philosophies behave like the cultural systems from which they originate.'[1] The centre of this typical conceptuality emerges in the concept of *culture*.

However, this concept is not brought to scientific definiteness, much less to philosophical evidence; rather, the concept of *culture* functions in a vague and multivalent ferment of ideas to guide all general reflection [*Besinnung*] on the totality of particular life-regions and on life as such. It has this overarching functional meaning because it has grown out of the spiritual claims of its century and is regarded by the latter as sufficient.

The two moments of its meaningful content, which approximate common contemporary usage, also characterize its *genuine provenance*. The contemporary [130] concept of culture includes first of all the moment of the '*historical*'. Culture is an historical phenomenon. The concepts of 'a people without culture' and 'a people without history' are taken as equivalent. The connection of the concept of culture with the idea of historicality – the formation of culture is an historical process – makes intelligible the conceptual domination of the concept of culture at the end of the nineteenth century: only where historical consciousness is awake can the idea of culture as process of formation and formative aim of human creative life penetrate into reflective consciousness. In going back to the driving forces that bring about the concept of culture as a conscious interpretative element of life, we are led to the idea of historical consciousness, the idea of historicality – and to the question of its genesis in intellectual history.

The second most frequently noticed moment of meaning in the historical concept of culture is '*achievement*', accomplishment, the realization of something valuable – and indeed always a significant, characteristic, outstanding achievement of value that bestows its stamp upon an historical age. At the end of the nineteenth century it is technology, and the theoretical foundation – *natural science* – that makes it possible, which counts as the specific achievement. We speak of the age of natural science, of the century of technology. To be sure, the natural sciences already had their first flowering in the seventeenth century, but their renewal in the nineteenth century, and their growing impact on the attitude of life as a whole, cannot be understood simply from the unbroken continuity of discovery and research in natural science.

That natural science became the pride of an epoch, the tendency of its consciousness, the idea of an *achievement* and therefore of culture, is explained only when we look into the genesis in intellectual history of the second substantive [131] moment of the historical concept of culture. If we can arrive at an unambiguous understanding of the historical motivations of the two initially conspicuous determinations of the historical concept of culture – 1) historical consciousness; 2) uncommon achievement of value (embodied in natural science and in the empirical sciences in general) – then we can understand the *typical* philosophy of the late nineteenth century.

For, so it is said, an age should come to self-consciousness in its philosophy. An age that sees itself as an achieving and culture-creating age therefore has as its philosophy a form of self-consciousness in which the idea of culture is dominant. Its philosophy is and calls itself '*philosophy of culture*'. In this, the historico-intellectual driving forces of the idea of historical culture and specific cultural achievement must, in a heightened degree, come to conceptual and structural expression.

If we trace intellectual history in its driving forces for the dominant power of the idea of culture in the nineteenth century, and particularly the motivations of the two indicated moments, this is to gain the intellectual perspective for the problematic that we will make accessible for renewed investigation. However, this examination of intellectual history, which must naturally be restricted to what is relevant to this problematic, is not to be taken just as an introduction in the sense of the usual historical preliminary considerations, simply in order to begin somewhere, because a beginning must be made. Rather, understanding the motives of intellectual history is *a genuine part of the preparation and appropriation of phenomenological critique.* (There is here a still deeper essential connection, which leads back to the essence of all phenomenological hermeneutics. [132] What suffices for our purposes is reference to a close connection between historical and 'systematic' examination – both are to be transcended!)

a) The Historical Concept of Culture. Enlightenment and Historical Consciousness

The first moment of the historical concept of culture in the nineteenth century is historical consciousness. The concept of culture itself goes back further, if only to the time of the eighteenth-century Enlightenment. To begin with, the word 'enlightenment' is not an historical category, but means something like civilization. Culture – *les nations les plus éclairées* – are for Pierre Bayle, Bossuet and Montesquieu the nations of culture as opposed to the peoples of nature. In the end, enlightenment refers to the typical culture of the eighteenth century, and the concept of enlightenment becomes a methodological category for chronological characterization by the science of history. The Enlightenment for the first time developed the idea of universal history with fundamental clarity. Such an idea was not at all alien to history, but had a peculiar relationship to it. This relationship was grounded in the absolute domination, at that time, of mathematical natural science and rational thought. These triumphs of pure thought expressed the ideal of the spirit as such, towards which every experience of mankind has to strive. The Enlightenment saw itself as the perfection of history on its way out of barbarism, superstition, deception and disorder.

The universal ideal of thought led to a broader vision extending beyond the nations. It grasped the solidarity of mankind, and saw progress towards enlightenment as the meaning of historical existence. Turgot discovered the law of the three stages in the development of mankind: the theological-mythical; the metaphysical; and the positive. (This was the law that Comte later made the basis of [133] his philosophy of history.) This Enlightenment conception of history, which resolves all historical events into conceptual connections, causes and intentions, conceptually clear goals, and which regards the individual as but an instance of the species, as an historical atom so to speak (thus the poets were valued not as figures within a genuine world of life-experience, but as perfecters of language who with their refinement and polish brought public and social life to an elevated level), disposes of the rich material made available by the sciences of the spirit [Geisteswissenschaften], which had begun a free and natural development in the sixteenthth and seventeenth centuries.

Kant too conceived history in terms of the Enlightenment, and culture meant (in its content dependent on the level of historical consciousness) the formation and perfection of mankind's rational determinations, rules and aims. With Herder, however, historical consciousness arrived at a decisive insight. Herder effected the change in that, under the influence of Hamann, he saw historical reality in its manifold irrational fullness, especially because he recognized the autonomous and unique value of each nation and age, each historical manifestation. Historical reality is no longer seen exclusively as a schematically regulated rationalist and linear direction of progress, which defines each stage only in so far as it overcomes barbarism and achieves rationality. In addition, the goal of progress is no longer an abstract rational happiness and virtuousness. Rather, 'every nation has its inherent midpoint of happiness, as every sphere its centre of gravity!'[2] Regard for [134] individual, qualitatively original centres and contexts of action. The category of 'ownness' [Eigenheit] becomes meaningful and is related to all formations of life, i.e. these for the first time become visible as such. Herder's intuitions receive, at one and the same time, their substantive broadening and philosophical grounding. Schlegel turned his attention to literatures and their historically original and autonomous forms. Research began into myths and legends. Beyond a mere declaration of their barbarism, one learned to see the beginnings of peoples as a proper stage of historical existence with its own value. From this new attitude, Niebuhr and Savigny examined the history of nations and laws. Schleiermacher saw for the first time the integrity and legitimacy of community life and the specificity of Christian consciousness of community. He discovered primordial Christianity and decisively influenced Hegel's youthful works on the history of religion, and indirectly also Hegel's specifically philosophical systematic, where the decisive ideas of the German movement reached their apex.

We thus come to the deepening that Herder's intuitions underwent from the side of philosophy. Kant stands at the boundary between the Enlightenment and German idealism, the most consistent and profound perfecter of the Enlightenment, and thereby already to some degree its overcomer. The displacement of the centre of gravity of all philosophical problematics in consciousness, subjectivity, the I of transcendental apperception, of theoretical and practical reason and the power of judgement, provides the impetus for Fichte's and Schelling's metaphysics of the ego. The historical in its individual multiplicity and uniqueness is now seen in terms of the creative deeds and activity of the subject, the self-worth of the person. Historical development pertains to consciousness and spirit. There, the first steps of spiritual development are to be discovered. The idea of developmental motives [135] and stages (phenomenology) of the spirit, and of the historical dialectic of reason, awakens. Hegel's so-called pan-logicism has its origin in the historical consciousness and is not a consequence of the simple radical theoretization of the theoretical! Alongside this philosophical development of historical consciousness runs the further development of empirical historical research, the grounding of philology, comparative linguistics, critical history of the Church, folk psychology and ethnology.

Ranke begins his work. The understanding of historical worlds, devotion to their richness and their movement, reach their perfection. He avoids any speculative dialectic, striving for the very core of the tale of world history in its genuine connection to universal history, thereby providing directions for the future. With the ever-accumulating empirical material of historical life, empirical mastery gains its priority and rank. The explanatory value of philosophical contextures of ideas, and of the construction of principles, dwindles, partly due to philosophy itself. The philosophers themselves, Trendelenburg, Erdmann, Zeller, Kuno Fischer, dedicate themselves to *history*, the tangible reality. An indignation over the insufficiency and erroneousness of all speculation pervades the intellectual world. The speculative enthusiasm of a Schelling in the philosophy of nature brings about a similar reaction in the area of natural science, with a turning-away from philosophy and an immersion in *experience*, the tangible reality. Pressing social and economic problems draw life completely on to the ground of experience and practical activity.

b) Culture as Accomplishment and Achievement [136]

The historically experiencing consciousness grasps the historical world – including its own period of the present – in its development, motivation, teleological formation and achievement. An age that is stirred by this consciousness sees its own life-aim in pressing forward to reality itself, to real Being. Its mastery in knowledge of every type and praxis of every form means that it hardly needs transcendent philosophical 'phantoms of the brain'.

With the motivation to develop the historical consciousness, which is the first moment of the culture concept, there emerges at the same time the second moment: the orientation of modern life to particular achievements in the area of practical empirical life, the development of technology in the widest sense. The decline of philosophical speculation and metaphysical construction reinforces enthusiasm for the empirical sciences, the mathematical as also the biological. (In so far as it was trapped in naturalism, the age did not find inappropriate a brash kind of metaphysical materialism, which found powerful support in England and France.)

§ 2. The Onset of the Problem of Value. The Overcoming of Naturalism by Lotze

To the extent that mid-nineteenth-century philosophy neither degenerated into naturalism nor fell back into the history of philosophy (this latter tendency, however, under the decisive influence of Hegel, was valuable and in some ways fundamental), it played a small influencing role in some conceptually weak [137] but still experientially genuine philosophies of speculative theism (Weiße, Ulrici *et al.*). The intellectual situation ensured that a primordial and thoroughgoing philosophical problematic came to the fore only with difficulty and gained force only by stages. The philosopher who experienced this liberation as necessary, and who actually attempted it, was *Hermann Lotze*.

Lotze was concerned to demonstrate (without, however, thereby relapsing into either the old ontological pre-critical metaphysics or the just superseded idealist metaphysics) the fundamental error of the absolute reification of the spirit promoted by naturalism, i.e. the reduction of all Being to corporeal matter, objectified events, matter and force, together with the refusal of all fundamental reflection.

This means positively: the discovery of a non-empirical, non-naturalistic, non-experiential sphere, of a non-sensory world, which, however, for all its non-sensoriness, avoids the extravagant naturalistic supra-sensoriness of the old metaphysics.

The eminent difficulty of this task, in a situation of intellectual history which we today can hardly experience in an originary manner, is indicated by the fact that Lotze only made a start at its solution. To be sure, Lotze had decisive intuitions, but he was always in danger of falling back into a speculative theological metaphysics, or into a too exclusive emphasis on natural reality.

Therefore a philosophical methodology did not sharply and clearly emerge, and the so-called 'systematic' orientation remained unstable, i.e. it avoided system while still striving for this. It did not achieve radical insight into the inner impossibility of a system of scientific philosophy. Nor did it have the ruthlessness to seize the experiential world and enclose it in a worldview system [138]. For genuine philosophy surely a 'hybrid', yet, when clarified in respect of its intellectual motivations and effects, understandable in its fruitfulness and distortions.

Lotze's overcoming of naturalism, and his simultaneous modified continuation of the tendencies of German idealism, were made possible by his conception of the central philosophical problems as problems of value, i.e. by their ultimate interpretation in a teleological context. Lotze did not see the problem of value in its full development, nor did he treat all problems with methodological rigour as problems of value. For both tasks beginnings can be found (particularly in *Microcosmos*[3] and the first writings). But his ubiquitous idea of the ought [*des Sollens*] and of value, and along these lines his interpretation of the Platonic ideas, which *are* not but instead *hold*, i.e. are valid as valuable, had a strong effect on the further development of philosophy, in the sense of a move away from naturalism and especially from psychologism. And if Lotze, in respect of epistemological problems, did not see clearly, and remained influenced by his training in the natural sciences, he also preserved, by reason of his origin in the German movement, a receptivity for the problematic of the transcendental *a priori*. The doctrine of the primacy of practical reason as 'value-sensing' [*wertempfindenden*] reason, which he took over from Fichte, became the decisive motif for the development of modern value-philosophy. In this, Lotze's position in intellectual history in the nineteenth century comes to its most pregnant expression: a safeguarding of the continuity and connection [139] with German idealism, but simultaneously a critical deflection of speculative idealism. To be sure, the pure idea of the transcendental is not fully elaborated, but with his conception of the *a priori* as the 'imitation of the innermost essence of the spirit',[4] as well as his grounding of logic in ethics, Lotze in principle overcomes naturalism, at the same time philosophically accommodating his empirically oriented age.

CHAPTER TWO
Windelband's Grounding of Modern Transcendental Philosophy of Value [140]

§ 3. Renewal of the Kantian Philosophy. The Character of Truth as Value

With this, however, the genesis, qualitative character and development of modern transcendental philosophy of value are not sufficiently explained. In the early 1870s, when Lotze's student Windelband qualified in Leipzig (with his 1873 work *On the Certainty of Knowledge*[1]), new and diverse autonomous approaches had already begun to take hold in philosophy. In 1871 there appeared Cohen's epoch-making book *Kant's Theory of Experience*, which determined the development of modern Neo-Kantianism. A year earlier Dilthey had brought out the first volume of his brilliant *Life of Schleiermacher* (1870), and in 1874 Brentano, with his work *Psychology from an Empirical Standpoint*, intervened in the philosophical research of that time.[2] Three quite different worlds of spiritual orientation and philosophical research, but each decisively determines Windelband's development and thereby modern philosophy of value; three spheres of influence, whose combined examination makes it possible to understand how transcendental philosophy of value [141] became the sole (serious) kind of philosophy of culture of the present.

By pointing to such intellectual motivations we do not mean to encourage the opinion that all intellectual phenomena of history can be grasped simply as the summative combination of stimuli and influences, without autonomous and original creative achievement. In the present case the separate emphasis and the emphasized separation of these motives have a far-reaching meaning, for we thereby grasp the fundamental groups of problems around which research on modern philosophy of value operates. A critical and positive phenomenological overcoming of philosophy of value, such as we strive for, must investigate these motives methodologically, because only in this way can the partial inauthenticity of these problems be fully understood.

a) The Rediscovery of the Transcendental Method by Cohen

Taking into consideration the three indicated spheres of influence, we shall now characterize the typical moments of value philosophy as they arise in the philosophical work of Windelband. To be sure, as coming from Lotze and Kuno Fischer, Windelband had a relation to the Kantian philosophy from the start. In other words, he was opposed to all naturalism. But it was Cohen's *Kant's Theory of Experience*, where the proper significance of Kant's *Critique of Pure Reason* was so to speak rediscovered, which first brought the rigorous and primordial meaning of the transcendental method, and of the transcendental as such, to the philosophical consciousness of that time. [142] In contrast to the then current psychological and physiological deformations of the Kantian theory of knowledge, Cohen saw the essential methodological connection between the problematic of the *Critique of Pure Reason* and the fact of mathematical natural science. The problem of knowledge does not concern the genetic physiologico-psychological process by which knowledge arises in individual human subjects, nor does it concern the reality of the external world. It is rather the objective methodological question concerning the structure of objectively given mathematical natural science. More precisely, it is the inquiry into the logical foundation of this knowledge, into the logical and categorial conditions of its possibility. The question is not about transcendent realities but about logical foundations. This question is not transcendent, but transcendental. The latter word characterizes the *methodological* character of the standpoint of the *Critique of Pure Reason*. It identifies the elements constituting the object of knowledge and sees objectivity as the connection between these elements, as the unity of the multiplicity of appearances. This unity itself is nothing other than the law, the rule of consciousness.

Beginning with such fundamental insights, Windelband made an autonomous intervention into this renewal of the Kantian philosophy, and under the immediate influence of Lotze gave a new form to the transcendental method. (When one speaks of Neo-Kantian schools today, one thinks primarily of the two renewals of the Kantian philosophy, inaugurated by Cohen and by Windelband.) The motives for Windelband's interpretation of Kant are mediated through Lotze and originate ultimately from Fichte, who, like German idealism in general, influenced Lotze especially in his early period. It thus becomes comprehensible why Fichte plays such an important role in the transcendental philosophy of value, so that one could almost characterize it as Neo-Fichteanism. [143] And indeed it is Fichte in his critical period (around the time 1794–1800) who held fast to Kant's transcendental idea and interpreted theoretical reason in the critical sense, as in essence practical. Thus Windelband's student Heinrich Rickert, from his own standpoint, rightly characterized Fichte as the 'greatest of all Kantians'.[3]

b) Practical Reason as the Principle of All Principles

The doctrine of the primacy of practical reason, the founding of theoretical scientific thought in practical belief and will to truth, became the fundamental philosophical conviction of the philosophy of value and conditioned its whole development into a more scientifically exact conception. In his first *Logic* (1843), Lotze emphasizes: 'As certain as it is that ultimate factical necessity can only be satisfactorily ascribed to what demands, and is capable of bearing, unconditional affirmation on account of its value for the moral spirit, so certain must it be for the final aim of philosophy to conceive the forms of logic and their laws not simply as factually present natural necessities of the spirit, but as appearances which derive from *another higher* root, and which derive their necessity from this.'[4]

Windelband already explicitly mentions in *On the Certainty of Knowledge* that Fichte had shifted the 'ethical motive' to the centre of all philosophy.[5] And thus Windelband too conceives [144] laws of thought as laws 'which thought *should* conform to, if it wants to become knowledge'.[6] 'The logical laws . . . are given to the soul as the norms which *should* direct and guide the effectiveness of natural law.' The logical law has 'normative *apriority*'.[7]

Windelband's interpretation of Kant is governed by his conviction that practical reason is the principle of all principles. Cohen's concise expression of the transcendental method, of the ways in which knowledge is founded, was carried further by Windelband through qualitative characterization of the underlying *a priori*. Whereas Cohen considers the *Critique of Pure Reason* more as a theory of experience, Windelband sees its task more as determining the *limits* of all science *vis-à-vis* the autonomy of the practical and moral world. At the same time, this strong emphasis on the practical affects the interpretation of the theoretical. The object is constituted by the *a priori* laws of scientific knowledge. The meaning of objectivity is the *law* of the constitution of objects: the object is the rule for representational connection. The rule has a normative character. The objectivity and truth of thought rest in its *normativity*. Theoretical philosophy 'is no longer to be a copy of the world, its task is to bring to consciousness the norms which first lend thought its value and validity'.[8] The final aim of such a philosophy lies in the spirit bringing to consciousness its normative law of theoretical comportment. It is thus immediately evident that the critique of knowledge covers only the smallest part of the self-consciousness of the spirit. [145] 'For there are other activities of the human spirit in which, independent of all knowledge, a consciousness of normative law-giving likewise shows that all value of individual functions is conditioned by certain rules, to which the individual movement of life is to be subordinated. Alongside normative thinking there stands normative willing and normative feeling: all three have the same entitlement.'[9] In all three *Critiques* taken together there is realized for the first time the comprehensive doctrine of the principles of reason. Philosophy must therefore be 'the total consciousness of the highest values of human life'.[10] Its problem is the validity of these values and norms; its method is not psychological-genetic, but *teleological*.[11] *Quaestio iuris*, not *quaestio factis*.[12]

With this interpretation of Kant, i.e. the emphasis on the value-character also of theoretical truth, it became possible for Windelband to bring all the problem-spheres of philosophy, the logical, ethical and aesthetic,[13] to a fundamental meaning (question concerning the normative consciousness) and already at an early stage to make precise the idea of philosophy as system and scientific worldview. The reason lies in the unbroken relation, mediated through the idea of value, to Fichte and the tradition of the great worldviews of German idealism. (The Marburg school, on the other hand, whose foundation was laid by Cohen in the work mentioned, remained for a long time exclusively occupied with positive work on the theoretical [146] foundation of the sciences, and only slowly and with difficulty became systematic. Cf. Natorp's appeal to Cohen in the 1918 lecture to the Kant society.[14])

c) Philosophy of Value as Critical Philosophy of Culture [146]

In the totality of spiritual life philosophy has a specific task that cannot be disputed by any empirical science, a task that fits into the character of nineteenth-century cultural consciousness, i.e. which avoids all exaggerated metaphysical speculation and seeks its firm foundation in experience. In universally valid values it possesses the systematic scientific framework, the field from which *culture* can be interpreted and obtain its own meaning. Philosophy of value is the authentic scientific philosophy of culture, which does not have the presumptuous ambition of creating new values, but interprets factually existing culture in terms of universally valid values. It is *critical* in so far as it 'examines the factual material of thought [in the given sciences], willing, feeling, with a view to universal and necessary validity'. 'Philosophy can become and remain an autonomous science only if it carries through the Kantian principle completely and purely.'[15] The philosophy of value is philosophy of culture as grounded in Kant's critical philosophy: it is transcendental philosophy of value, *'critical science of universally valid values'*.[16]

[147] Windelband's early development – and thus that of value philosophy – links up with the process of renewal of the Kantian philosophy, which process was made scientific through Cohen. The characteristic of Windelband's Kant interpretation: primacy of practical reason; theoretical reason: rule, norm, value; philosophy: critical science of universally valid values.

However, it is not a matter of slavishly following Kant. Especially with the growing penetration of empirical psychology into the philosophical problematic it is a matter of grounding philosophy from the matter itself [*Sache selbst*], and without historical dependencies, as a critical science of universally valid values.

A grounding of philosophy will always begin in the theoretical sphere, in the theory of knowledge, logic in the broadest sense. Does this region contain basic knowledge of the sort that founds a systematic structure, such that the idea of value can be the first principle of the systematic contexture? Windelband sees such an epistemological foundation in the distinction between *judgement [Urteil]* and *evaluation [Beurteilung]*.

To be examined: 1) as theoretical means for the universal foundation of value philosophy and its demarcation from other sciences; 2) its implications for the special advancement of specifically logical epistemological problems.

§ 4. Judgement and Evaluation [148]

a) The Grounding of the Distinction between Judgement and Evaluation by Brentano

Thus, through returning to motivations of intellectual history, the object of these phenomenologico-critical considerations is given a preliminary and rough outline. It is now a matter, keeping in mind the two above-mentioned philosophical driving forces, Brentano and Dilthey, of following the further substantive concrete expressions of the tendencies of value philosophy within Windelband's development.

Windelband himself is convinced that this critical science of universally valid values 'is nothing other than the comprehensive execution of Kant's basic idea',[17] but also that the necessity of such a special science can be demonstrated 'without the formulas of the Kantian doctrine'. Windelband provides this purely systematic grounding of philosophy of value in his essay 'What is Philosophy?' (1882).

The possibility of thus systematically grounding philosophy as science of value rests on the extremely important *'distinction between judgement and evaluation'*. The elaboration and grounding of this fundamental distinction, which in the end lays the ground for transcendental philosophy of value, depends on *taking over* and *reworking Franz Brentano*'s basic insights. I am especially emphasizing the significance of this second driving force for the development of value-philosophy, and for *two reasons*. In the first place the value-philosophy of Windelband, initially also that of Rickert, seriously underestimates the influence of Brentano. In the early period at least, [149] it is not expressly admitted, but rather alluded to in passing, that 'from the psychological side', 'although in baroque form', Brentano drew attention to this distinction.[18] Instead, reference is made to Sigwart and Bergmann. Incidentally, Sigwart makes precisely the opposite judgement concerning this purported priority.[19]

Rickert repeats this judgement of Windelband in his 1892 *Object of Knowledge*.[20] However, a noteworthy reversal occurs in the third edition of 1915, where Brentano is suddenly no longer just mentioned in passing but expressly treated in the text, indeed with the introductory sentence: 'Doubtless Brentano, who treated our question in depth and clearly showed that judgement is not representation, renders great service in this respect.'[21] If I refer to these things, it is not just because of a dispute over priority. The matter itself requires a genuine understanding of the development of philosophy of value to which Rickert himself is driven, as his reversal demonstrates. The second reason for explicitly emphasizing Brentano's influence is closely connected with this.

The indicated distinction between judgement and evaluation is not only adopted by Windelband from Brentano as the central distinction for a first exposition of the idea of philosophy of value, but also grounds Windelband's investigations on logic in his 'Contributions to the Doctrine of Negative Judgement' and in his essay 'On the System of Categories'.[22] The former work [150] had a decisive effect on subsequent systematic epistemological research within the value philosophy of Rickert and his student Lask, who go quite beyond Windelband. Rickert and Lask employed the distinction within a philosophy of value for a treatment of the epistemological problem of transcendence as such, and also, since the latter is the foundation of all philosophy, for grounding the most recent problematic of value-philosophy.[23]

Since on the one hand our critico-phenomenological considerations relate to the systematically much more rigorous handling of the problem by Rickert and Lask, while on the other hand Husserl, the discoverer of the phenomenological problematic and method, is a student of Brentano, who knew nothing of phenomenology and also did not later embrace it, I hold, on the basis of intellectual history and for systematic reasons, that a consideration of some relevant insights of Brentano is indispensable. In this way, right at the common origin, the qualitatively different motivations exerted by Brentano, and the divergent directions of research, become comprehensible. I therefore treat the characteristic opposition between philosophy of value and Brentano up to the point where I pass over from intellectual history to critical phenomenological research of fundamental problems.

b) Judgement and Validity (Windelband) [151]

We now consider more closely Windelband's distinction between judgement and evaluation, in its meaning for the general foundation of value philosophy and with respect to his treatment of purely logical problems relating to judgement and the categories. In the following I first give a simple exposition without critical comment, but so arranged as to have an inner systematic connection to what follows. (It is worth mentioning that I cannot make Windelband's account more intelligible than he has himself.)

'All propositions in which we express our insights are distinguished, despite apparent grammatical equivalence, into two precisely demarcated classes: judgements [*Urteile*] and evaluations [*Beurteilungen*].' Something fundamentally different is 'expressed' in both cases: in judgements the 'belonging together of two representational contents', in evaluations a 'relation of judging consciousness to the represented object' (the hidden intentionality, which lies in the expressed judgement). Although in the two sentences 'This thing is white' and 'This thing is good', the grammatical form is completely identical, there is a fundamental difference between them, and indeed the one indicated.[24]

The general predicative relation is in both cases the same. What is different is the predicate. The judgement predicate is a 'ready-made determination taken from the content of the objective representation', the predicate of the evaluation is 'a relation referring to a goal-setting consciousness'.[25] In evaluation there is expressed the feeling of approval or disapproval, 'with which the judging consciousness relates to the represented object'. Evaluative predicates are [152] 'expressions of approval or displeasure' (a concept is true or false, an act is good or bad, etc.). Evaluation does not substantively widen objective knowledge; the latter must already be presented as 'finished' before it makes sense to evaluate it.[26] The evaluative predicate does not lie in the subject; it is only attributed to the subject by reference to a measure: purpose. 'Every evaluation presupposes as measure of itself a particular purpose, and has meaning and significance only for whoever recognizes this purpose.'[27]

All propositions of knowledge are already a combination of judgement and evaluation; they are representational connections whose truth-value is decided by affirmation or denial.[28] The pure theoretical judgement, the connection of representations unaffected by evaluation, occurs only in questions and in the so-called problematical judgement.[29]

With the help of this distinction the object and method of philosophy can be sharply demarcated from the other sciences. The mathematical, the descriptive and explanatory sciences *seek to establish the entire range of content of what is to be affirmed*, the concrete propositions of knowledge that *realize* the affirmations. In this region there is no place left for philosophy; it is not mathematical, or descriptive, or explanatory. Windelband even protests in the name of the Kantian philosophy against the 'superficial opinion' which takes psychological results as philosophy. What remains curious, however, is that Windelband takes his fundamental distinction from [153] a 'psychology *from an empirical standpoint*'!

Its particular object is the evaluations themselves, but not as objects for consideration by empirical science. 'That is the concern of psychology and the history of culture.'[30] Evaluations are 'simply there' as empirical facts, not at all to be distinguished from other psychical or physical objects. But – and this is the 'fundamental fact of philosophy' – we are convinced 'that there are certain evaluations *which are absolutely valid, even if they are not in fact universally accepted and acknowledged as such*'.[31] Every evaluation of a representational connection as true presupposes an absolute standard valid for all. 'The same thing applies in the ethical and aesthetic domains.'[32] The claim to absolute validity distinguishes itself from all the thousand evaluations of individual feeling, the so-called hedonistic evaluations.[33] 'No one presupposes general validity for his feelings of pleasure or displeasure.'[34] Corresponding to the three forms of evaluation claiming absolute validity there are three basic philosophical disciplines: logic, ethics and aesthetics. In these the claim of universal validity, as found in factical knowledge, is to be 'tested'.[35] Through 'what philosophical procedure' is the 'critical testing' to be carried out? Philosophy, according to what has been said, is not mathematical, or descriptive, or explanatory!

One must first become clear (!) about the presupposed *universal validity*. It does not [154] have a factical character. It is quite irrelevant how many people actually acknowledge a truth; universal validity is an ideal that *should* be.[36]

In addition 'the *necessity* with which we feel the validity of logical, ethical and aesthetic determinations' is not a causal necessity, not a factual 'cannot be otherwise', but a necessity of the ought, a 'not allowed to be otherwise'.[37] Philosophy has to 'establish' the principles of logical, ethical and aesthetical judgings[38] (thus to 'test' critically the claim, the criteria of statements of validity). But one does not discover 'a criterion of what is supposed to be valid' (unclear!) through research of psychology and cultural history into factically existing evaluations. On the other hand we are all convinced, 'we all believe . . . that . . . there is an entitlement of what is necessary in the higher sense, which *should* be valid for all'.[39] Everywhere, accordingly, where empirical consciousness 'discovers in itself' this ideal necessity of the ought, 'it comes upon a *normative consciousness*'.[40] Philosophy is 'reflection [*Besinnung*] on this normative consciousness, as the scientific investigation into which particular determinations of content and forms of empirical consciousness have the value of normative consciousness'.[41] As the science of normative consciousness, whose recognition is its presupposition, it 'researches' (?) 'empirical [!] consciousness in order to establish [!] at which points that normative universal validity emerges'.[42] 'Consciousness in general' is therefore a system of the norms which first make possible universally valid evaluations.[43]

[155] In the last sentence, with the help of the aforesaid distinction, the reinterpretation of Kant by value philosophy comes to unmistakable expression, and at the same time it becomes clear how the distinction founds and directs the systematic blueprint of philosophy of value. The possibility of carrying through the systematic of philosophy of value depends on taking truth as a value and taking theoretical knowledge as a practical activity bound by a norm. Therefore the solidity of this foundation proves itself above all in value-philosophy's treatment of logical problems. In this direction Windelband's treatise on negative judgement has become important for the further development of value-philosophy. It too depends on the distinction between judgement and evaluation. I shall give a short account of the essential points.

c) Windelband's Treatise on Negative Judgement: Scientific Determination of the Forms of Judgement

With Lotze and Sigwart, Windelband sees the insufficiency of Kantian formal logic in its dogmatic adoption of the forms of judgement from traditional Aristotelian school logic. Alongside this there stands, unmediated, the new transcendental logic, i.e. material as opposed to formal logic, an epistemological logic whose new insights were in some degree distorted by the circumstance that Kant uncritically 'reads off' the categories, as the fundamental transcendental elements, from the underlying table of judgements. 'He deprived the analytical forms of general logic of all substantive force of knowledge . . . on the other hand he credited the synthetic forms of transcendental logic with the same constitutive value for the total world of appearance which the old metaphysics credited to the analytical forms for the things in themselves.'[44] A reform of logic, therefore, has the task of [156] establishing the true connection between formal and transcendental logic, which can occur only if the fundamental phenomena of logic, the *judgements*, are correctly conceived.

'Logic is the doctrine of judgement.'[45] From here, from the close connection between doctrine of judgement and doctrine of categories as laid down in the *Critique of Pure Reason*, the rationale for Windelband's further contribution to logic can be understood.[46] One main concern of the doctrine of judgement, the 'cardinal question', is the table of judgements, i.e. the division of judgements, the question concerning the *'principium divisionis'*.[47] One old viewpoint is that of quality: the division of judgements into affirmative and negative.

Windelband wants to make his distinction between judgement and evaluation fruitful for the scientific determination of qualitatively different forms of judgement, and in this way to advance a crucial problem of logic. He refers to the way in which the new logic (Sigwart, Lotze, Bergmann), in opposition to metaphysical objectification, increasingly recognizes *negation* as a *subjective* phenomenon, as a 'form of relation of consciousness' and not a real relation in the sense of separation. Sigwart interprets the negative judgement as 'rejection' of the attempted or possible 'corresponding positive' – accordingly the negative judgement 'a is not b' is a double judgement, meaning that 'the judgement, a is b, is false'.[48] Here Windelband introduces his distinction. The negative judgement is not another judgement (this conception would lead to an infinite regress), but an evaluation, therefore not a representational connection in which the predicate 'invalid' would appear, but a judgement *'about* the truth-value* [*Wahrheitswert*] of a [157] judgement',[49] an evaluation in respect of . . . 'false' is not a content of a representation, but a relation: the attitude of consciousness to a content. And Windelband characterized the *evaluation* as 'the reaction of a willing and feeling consciousness to a determinate representational content'.[50] A practical comportment accordingly, and as such alternative. 'The logical value-judgement of representations which occurs in the judgement [is] located within the practical side of the life of the soul and . . . the value of truth is coordinated to the other values. The disjunction of true and false, the alternate relation of evaluation of representations concerning truth-value, is the psychological [!] fundamental fact of logic.'[51]

Affirmative judgement and negative judgement are 'co-ordinated types'. The question now arises as to 'whether *still other forms are to be placed alongside them'*. To decide this, one must keep in mind 'the relationship of the activity of evaluation to the functions of feeling and willing'. 'As every feeling is either of pleasure or displeasure, as every willing is either desire [!] or revulsion [!], so is every judgement either affirmation or denial.' But from this comparison there follows still more. 'Like all functions of approval or rejection', evaluation has 'the possibility of a graduated difference'. 'The "feeling of conviction"(or of "certainty") is, like all feelings, susceptible of gradations.' Thus the concept of *probability* becomes intelligible. Certainty is to be conceived as a 'state of feeling'.[52] Every logical evaluation has a certainty, a feeling of conviction, in itself.

The gradation in the intensity of certainty applies just as much to the negative as to the positive judgement. Both can be regarded as [158] the two 'end-points of complete certainty', which through gradual reduction approach a 'point of indifference' where neither affirmation nor denial occurs. This *zero-point of logical evaluation* is 'of great significance for the doctrine of quality of judgements'. For it also is not unambiguous. 'The indifference . . . between positive and negative reaction can . . . be *total or it can be critical.*'[53]

Total indifference occurs where nothing at all is judged, with all 'representational processes' which happen without reference to truth-value; logic does not take these in any way into account, for logical investigations always presuppose 'the relation of representational connections to the evaluation of truth'.[54] Only the *question* belongs here; in it the representational connection is realized. It is brought into relation to truth-evaluation, *but the latter is not itself carried out.* The question contains the theoretical component of the judgement but not the practical component; it is representational connection with the demand for a decision on truth-value.[55] The question is the *preliminary stage* of the judgement, if one sees its nature in the evaluation (decision on value). (It is itself a judgement and co-ordinated to affirmation and negation, if like Lotze one sees the essence of judgement in the representational connection.) It is otherwise with critical indifference, which has already gone through the question and where neither sufficient reasons for denial nor sufficient reasons for affirmation have been given. This 'state of uncertainty' finds expression in the 'so-called problematical judgement'. The judgement that 'a can be b' is equivalent in value to 'a can be not-b' is then really problematical if it means that nothing should be said (!) about the validity of the representational connection $a = b$. [159] Like the question, the problematical judgement contains the theoretical moment of the judgement: 'the realized representational connection, but at the same time an explicit *suspension of evaluation*'. Unlike the question, the problematical judgement is 'a real act of knowledge'. For in it there is affirmed that nothing is to be asserted!! Dispensing with decision is itself 'a complete decision'![56] Only it is questionable whether there is something *essentially new*. It is a taking of an attitude towards the taking of an attitude! With respect to quality, there are therefore affirmative, negative, problematical judgements; at the same time the position of the question is clarified. Judgements: representational *connection*, whose truth-value is to be decided through evaluation. *Relation – quality.*

§ 5. Contribution to the Doctrine of Categories: Logic as Doctrine of Relation: Reflexive and Constitutive Categories

We have still briefly to consider Windelband's contribution to the doctrine of categories. In treating Windelband's Kant interpretation we heard that objectivity constitutes itself in a rule of representational connection, *synthesis*.[57] According to Windelband, ever since Kant's *Critique of Pure Reason*, this concept is 'the fundamental principle of all theoretical philosophy'.[58] Consciousness can virtually be defined as the function of relation. Even the poorest and simplest impressions always contain a 'unified multiplicity'.[59] The activities of thought (also sensory representation) consist 'in a representation or assertion of relations between [160] a more or less extended multiplicity of separated moments'. The relations are 'something different' from the separate and linked contents, and are therefore not derivative, but on the other hand in their application they are indeed dependent on the contents. The forms of relation are made independent from the contents *through reflection*; however, in real application it depends on *the contents* 'in which relations they may or should be posited through the synthetic consciousness'.[60]

'In these distinctively complicated relations and dependencies between forms and contents of consciousness there are hidden the deepest and most difficult problems of transcendental psychology and epistemology.' Thus Windelband wants to highlight the central position of synthesis in the totality of the problematic of transcendental philosophy, and by an *'outline for the system of categories'* to make comprehensible why he proceeds from this centre.[61]

Windelband understands by *'categories'* nothing else but these synthetic forms of consciousness, 'the relations, in which intuitively given contents are bound together through synthesizing consciousness'. In the judgement, subject and predicate are put in relation by the categories and the truth-value of this relation is expressed. 'The judgement decides on whether this relation "is valid".' (A concept is knowledge only in a finished judgement.) In this way the task of logic concentrates on the systematic relational connection, 'on the doctrine of the relation'.[62]

Windelband seeks in this, alongside quality, the only important differentiating ground for judgements.[63]

The viewpoint of 'modality' belongs to quality, that of quantity does not at all belong in pure logic, but is [161] very important for methodology. What then is the principle for the system of categories? This question is necessary, for it cannot be simply a matter of the accidental empirical bundling together of categories.

'The changing processes of synthetic thought teach us' that the relational function of thought, and the representations which form its content, have among themselves a 'free mobility'; various contents can enter into the same relation, and the same relation can stand in various relations. Therefore, when one speaks of the 'relation of consciousness to Being, this means independence of the content of consciousness from the function of consciousness'. This is the meaning of the category 'Being' [Sein].[64]

'The facts of memory confirm – seen from inner experience – that the content of representation is independent of the function, which is able variously to direct itself upon it, to abandon it, and again to apprehend it.'[65] This proposition is again typical of the crude and unmethodological kind of 'transcendental psychology' which does not see genuine problems.

From this articulation of consciousness and Being – which precisely overlooks 'Being' in its specific character as consciousness and experience! – there emerges for Windelband a fundamental distinction which in the simplest way conditions the system of categories in its structure. With the 'addition of the function of consciousness to the independent contents' just those relations (as their forms – the categories) can be valid which apply to the contents themselves – which are 'taken up and repeated' by consciousness – or such as enter into the content only because they are brought into it by consciousness. In the first case the categories have [162] objective, in the second case only represented (properly understood: subjective) validity. The inherence relation counts as real, but not that of simple equivalence or difference, e.g. between colour and sound. 'It never belongs to the real Being of a content to be the same as or different from another content.'[66] They 'get' into this relation only through consciousness itself.

So two main groups of categories emerge: the reflexive and the constitutive. The reflexive lead back to the 'combining activities' (reflection) of consciousness, the constitutive signify *substantive* connections of representational elements. The reflexive form presents the immanent nature of consciousness most purely, whereas 'the constitutive relational forms are collectively modified through the transcendental relation to the independent "Being" of contents'.[67]

I will not enter into the more detailed derivation of the individual categories of both groups. What should be kept in view is just the distinction of form and content, its interpretation in terms of consciousness, and its function as the principle of category derivation. In the essay 'Logic', Windelband gives an overview of the development of logic in the nineteenth century since Kant. There is nothing to add to what has so far been presented, apart from the reference to 'the emphasis on the methodological side of logic'.[68] The renewal of the Kantian philosophy, above all by the Marburgers, who for the first time seriously interpreted the *Critique of Pure Reason* as theory of science and whose services Windelband treats somewhat as a side-issue, brought about an intensive treatment of the methodological problems (Windelband mentions above all Sigwart and [163] Lotze). Windelband thereby totally ignores the services of *Dilthey*, who, not so much from the Kant renewal as from deeper origins, from a continuity with the German movement (especially Schleiermacher) and the development of historical consciousness, took up in a comprehensive way the problem of a critique of historical reason – more than a decade before Windelband held his much cited 1894 Straßburg rectoral address on 'history and natural science'.

§ 6. The Inclusion of the Problem of History in Philosophy of Value

We thus come to the third decisive motive for the nature and direction of development of modern transcendental philosophy of value, more accurately for the problem of history, which in several ways plays a role in it. By taking up *this* problem we can understand how precisely the system of value philosophy develops into modern culture-philosophy κατ᾽ ἐξοχήν. I first give a general characterization of the intentions of Dilthey, by whom Windelband was doubtless influenced, albeit apparently in a contrary sense.

The spiritual personality of Dilthey stands in unbroken continuity with that complex of human sciences created by the historical school – in the comprehensive sense of Herder and Winckelmann through to Wolf, Niebuhr, Savigny, Grimm, Humboldt, Schleiermacher, Boeckh,

Ranke – which has thereby grown into the spiritual world of German idealism.

a) Natural Sciences and Human Sciences. Dilthey's Founding of a Descriptive Psychology [164]

The awakening of historical consciousness, its emancipation from the supervision of the natural sciences and metaphysics, is nothing else but the first genuine sighting of the fundamental characteristic growth of *all* human facts. From this emancipation there arises the further basic task of authentic philosophical founding. Comte and John Stuart Mill sought to solve the puzzle of historical consciousness and the human sciences by reference to the context of the natural sciences; an attempt which was immediately felt to be misconceived by researchers in the human sciences, despite the fact that these researchers themselves possessed no genuine philosophical means for refuting the methodological dogmatism of natural science. From the situation of the developing historical sciences of the spirit, from the context of living reality, value and purpose, Dilthey sought in his *Introduction to the Human Sciences* (1883)[69] to present the autonomous position of the human sciences *vis-à-vis* the natural sciences, to uncover the epistemological and logical context of the former, and to validate the significance of the singular.

Decisive is therefore the 'self-reflection' [*Selbstbesinnung*][70] of the spirit, 'the study of the forms of spiritual life through description'.[71] 'Only in self-reflection do we discover within us the unity of life and its continuity, which sustain and preserve all these relations.'[72] In this way we can arrive at principles and propositions to ground the construction of the historical world [165] in the human sciences. The basic sciences are anthropology and psychology, but not in the explanatory, hypothesis-forming sense of the methodology of natural science. What is meant, rather, is psychology as descriptive science[73] of a kind which must first be created. Dilthey struggled with this problem for his whole life, and we are indebted to him for valuable intuitions, which, however, do not reach down to ultimate and primordial principles and to radical purity and novelty of method. Phenomenology, whose basic founding he of course did not live through, but the far-reaching meaning of whose first breakthroughs and researches he was one of the first to recognize, is now beginning to fulfil the secret longing of his life. Although he was no logician, he saw, in one stroke and with brilliant spiritual power of feeling, the significance of the (at that time) misunderstood and hardly noticed *Logical Investigations* of Husserl (cf. Husserl's course in this semester on 'Nature and Spirit').

Dilthey already saw clearly (1883) the meaning of the singular and unique in historical reality; he recognized that it had a 'quite different meaning' in the human sciences than in the natural sciences. In the latter it is only 'a tool' for analytical generalization; in history it is *'aim'* and purpose. The historian seeks the universal of human things in the *particular*. 'Were the conditions for the knowledge of nature in the same sense foundational for the construction of the human sciences . . . then the separation of the foundation of the human sciences from that of the natural sciences would be without any point.'[74]

b) Windelband's Distinction between Sciences of Law and Sciences of Event. Nomothetic and Idiographic Thinking [166]

Taking up the foundational work of Dilthey, Windelband seeks to give this methodological problem a new turn, without, however, in any way going into Dilthey's position and its crucial ideas. Windelband starts by criticizing the opposition between nature and spirit. He sees this as a substantive rather than a methodological opposition, an opposition between substantively different *objects*. He finds that this division remains fixed in the general mode of representation and expression, i.e. is pre-scientific and naively dogmatic, thus by no means so sure and self-evident 'that it can without further ado be made into the foundation of a classification'.[75] Above all, this substantive opposition does not coincide with the modes of knowledge. For psychology as the fundamental science of the spirit works in the attitude and method of natural science, and on the other hand the separation of nature and spirit is supposed to found the methodological separation between natural and spiritual sciences. 'A division which involves such difficulties does not have systematic permanence.'[76] The methodological demarcation between natural science and history must follow a different procedure.

Closer consideration shows the 'logical equivalence' of psychology with the natural sciences in their formal aim of knowledge. They both seek *laws of an occurrence*, whether the occurrence be a movement of bodies, a transformation of material, a development of organic life, or a process of representation, willing and feeling.[77]

[167] By contrast, the sciences 'which one usually describes as human sciences', are oriented to the occurrence of a unique temporally bounded

reality and to its exhaustive presentation. Structures of human life – heroes and peoples, languages, religions, codes of law, literatures, art, sciences – are to be presented in their 'unique reality'.

It is possible to arrive at a pure methodological principle for the division of sciences, namely 'the formal character of the aim of knowledge'.[78] Some seek general laws, others 'particular historical (!) facts'. Expressed in formal-logical terms: in one group of sciences the aim is apodictic judgement, the other group aims at the assertoric proposition. As sciences of experience, both are grounded in the establishment of facts, in perception.[79] However, their logical aims are different. In the one case 'the general in the form of natural law', in the other case 'the individual in historically (!) determined form'. The first are sciences of law, the second are sciences of events. Scientific thought in the natural sciences is *nomothetic*, in the sciences of history it is *idiographic*.[80] This 'logical' division therefore excludes from the beginning the problem of a *descriptive* psychology. It recognizes psychology only as natural science, which makes development of the methodological problem considerably easier.

The presentation of the three motives of intellectual history (and in the narrower sense, of the history of philosophy), along with the fundamental meaning of German idealism and Lotze in their influence on Windelband's philosophical work, has now been concluded. Windelband's efforts for 'systematic philosophy' have been characterized to the extent that we can now understand the further intensive systematic, predominantly epistemological development [168] and deeper founding of the system of transcendental philosophy of value carried out by Windelband's student Rickert, and by the latter's student Lask.

In the present context it is not necessary to go into Windelband's well-known contributions to the history of philosophy. An easily comprehensible systematic presentation of Windelband's origins, works, the teachings and the teacher, has been published by Rickert on the occasion of his teacher's death.[81] A comparison of this small work with what has been presented above should show that I see the motivations of intellectual history very differently and, I am convinced, more correctly.

CHAPTER THREE

The Further Development of Value-Philosophy by Rickert [169]

§ 7. Historical Formation of Concepts and Scientific Knowledge: Reality as Heterogeneous Continuum

I take up the development of transcendental value philosophy at the point where it left us standing, the *problem of history*. Rickert took up the basic elements of Windelband's rectoral address, put them methodologically on a broader philosophical basis and formulated the problem: *The Limits of Formation of Concepts in Natural Science: a Logical Introduction to the Historical Sciences*, Part One in 1896, Part Two in 1902. In between, by way of preparation of Part Two, was *Cultural Science and Natural Science*, 1899 (second edition 1910, third edition 1915). The second edition of *Limits* was in 1913. In addition, there was the essay on the general problem of historical science, published in the *Festschrift* for Kuno Fischer (second edition 1907): 'Philosophy of History'. In these works Rickert brought the problem of the philosophy of history into systematic relation with the fundamental questions of epistemology, at the same time leading the problem of history into the ultimate questions of system and worldview of scientific philosophy of *culture*. Since our critical phenomenological consideration concerns the basic standpoints of epistemology and of the *system of value*, I will not further examine these works on the history of philosophy. Husserl, in his lecture-course 'Nature and Spirit', admittedly not by way of critique but through positive development of his phenomenological research, will give information in this area.

[170] What distinguishes the treatment by value philosophy of the problem of the history of philosophy is its emphasis on the

methodological character of the question. Not the substantive opposition between nature and spirit, but the formal-methodological opposition of the goals of knowledge, is decisive. Rickert, whose logical and dialectical talent is far superior to that of Windelband, conceives this idea more precisely as the problem of *concept-formation*. The aim of the empirical sciences is the scientific treatment of reality by means of the concept Therefore the difference between sciences must ultimately arise in their formation of concepts, i.e. in the various ways by which individual features and elements of concepts are apprehended and joined. This process depends on the goal that scientific knowledge sets, on what is posited as the principle of concept-formation.

Rickert seeks something – 'a logical introduction to the historical sciences' – which did not emerge in Windelband's sketchy positive characterization of historical science (the latter emphasizes the idiographic, the presentation of individual form; connection with artistic presentation). He seeks the *principle* of *historical* concept-formation by reference to the 'limits of concept-formation in natural science'. In this contraposition 'nature' is not conceived as material, as the world of bodies or physical being, but rather in formal-methodological terms, in the sense of Kant's transcendental philosophy: nature as 'the being of things, *in so far* as they are determined by universal laws'.[1]

The reference here is to an epistemological founding of the methodological principle that grounds the distinction [171] between the two groups of sciences. It is thus necessary, before anything definite can be said about scientific knowledge in particular sciences and special methods, to determine the meaning of the concept of scientific knowledge '*in general*'.

If scientific knowledge is set the task of depicting and describing reality as it is, then this is immediately seen to be an impossible undertaking, for reality is an 'incalculable multiplicity' which cannot be mastered by concepts. Whatever content of reality can be taken up by concepts is vanishingly small compared with what remains. It is also said that reality is irrational compared with rational concepts and cannot be captured by the latter without something being left over. There are old sayings: everything flows, physical as well as psychical being has the character of continuous transition; *all of reality is a continuum*.[2] In addition there is a second moment of reality: no part of reality is absolutely identical with another. Every reality shows its own unique characteristic individual mark. There is nothing absolutely homogeneous; everything is different, *everything real is heterogeneous.* In sum, reality is a *heterogeneous continuum.* This togetherness of continuity and alterity gives reality that character of irrationality before which the concept is quite powerless. If a descriptive depiction must be dispensed with, then the only possibility is a re-forming of reality through the concept, and we must discover 'how the concept attains *power over the real'.*[3] This is possible only through a conceptual separation of continuity and alterity. [172] The continuum can be grasped only when it becomes *homogeneous.* The heterogeneous becomes conceptualizable, as soon as the continuum is transformed into a discretum. Thus two diametrically opposed ways of concept formation are revealed: reality as heterogeneous continuum can be transformed into a homogeneous continuum or into a heterogeneous discretum.

But in order that such a conceptual re-forming of reality is not arbitrary, a principle of selection is needed; this determines which essential moments of reality will enter into the concept, and which will be excluded as inessential. These principles of concept-construction are clearly dependent on the aim that the sciences have set for their cognitive work.

According to Rickert, the first signs of a specific concept-formation can already be seen in the verbal meanings of ordinary language. Verbal meanings, e.g. 'tree', are general; they refer to reality not in respect of an individual instance, but by omission of individual characteristics. The concept of 'tree' means something common to all trees. The sciences aim at such general concepts, at bringing together conceptual elements into ultimate general concepts and laws. In this way reality is conceptually mastered, natural knowledge is generalized. Is there now alongside this principle of generalizing concept-formation something formally different, which separates essential from inessential in a totally different way? In fact there are sciences that are not oriented towards the establishment of general laws of nature and the formation of general concepts: the *historical* sciences. They want to present reality in its individuality and uniqueness, an undertaking for which the general concept of natural science, which precisely excludes the individual as inessential, is not at all suited. [173] The science of history does not *want* to generalize – this is the decisive point for its logic. Its concept-formation is individualizing, and so it can already be said: *'Reality becomes nature when we consider it with respect to the universal, it becomes history when we consider it with respect to the particular and individual.'*[4] How is history, if it is to present the unique, particular and individual, to be possible as science?

§ 8. The Question Concerning the Possibility of the Science of History

What is it actually that we wish to understand and know in this historical individualizing way? Natural processes interest us only as particular cases of a general law, not with respect to their individuality and uniqueness. The latter interest pertains only to realities to which *values* are attached. We call such realities, objects and values, to which there are attached values recognized by human beings, *objects of culture*. Those objects, on the other hand, which are free from this reference to values, we see as nature. The cultural meaning of an object consists precisely in its uniqueness, in its distinctiveness *vis-à-vis* other objects. Therefore, only individualizing concept-formation is faithful to the cultural process in its value relatedness. An inner connection between culture and history shows itself. This becomes still more significant when it appears that the *concept of culture* first makes history possible as science. The concept of culture makes possible individualizing concept-formation, so that a 'depictable individuality' is highlighted, for not every moment of a cultural object is interesting enough to be depicted [174] (also not all determinations which it has in common with others). For the historian there are essential and inessential aspects of reality. There are historically meaningful individualities and meaningless differences; from the incalculable totality of individual things the historian only considers that which 'incorporates a cultural value or stands in relation to it'. The concept of culture provides the principle for picking out the historically essential from the historically inessential. 'Through the *values* which attach to culture the concept of a representable historical individuality is first *constituted*.'[5] Individualizing concept-formation of history is a '*value-relating procedure*'. This concept of '*value-relation*' must be understood as a '*theoretical* concept', and must not be confused with decisions, with value-judgements, on whether things are or are not valuable.[6] To be 'related to values' does not mean 'evaluating'. These are two totally different acts. 'The theoretical *value-relation* remains in the region of the *establishment of facts*, not however the practical valuing.' (Which means?!) 'Valuing must always be *praise* or *blame* value-*relatedness* is *neither* of these.'[7]

Cultural values must be presupposed as generally recognized if historical concept-formation is to have objectivity and universal validity by relation to them. Or is recognition of values, through which historical concept-construction occurs, simply factical, itself historically variable, restricted to a particular sphere of culture, so that the objectivity of history ical science is only apparent and of minimal value compared with the natural sciences? Must not rather cultural values, if they are to guarantee genuine scientific objectivity, *be valid* 'irrespective of their factical application'?[8] [175] The objectivity of cultural science is therefore dependent on the unity and objectivity of a *system of valid values*. The necessity arises of *grounding* this validity of values. Natural science too, however 'value-free' its concept-formation and methodology, presupposes the value of truth and thus makes inevitable the problem of the validity of value and systematics of value.

It has emerged, therefore, that these methodological investigations in their point of origin, the doctrine of concept-formation, lead to the basic problem: the relation between concept and reality, the epistemologically fundamental problem that the same investigations in their end-goal, the grounding of the objectivity of sciences, refer to the universal problem of value. Rickert undertook the epistemological problem of reality in his first important publication (*Habilitation*), and it has occupied him ever since. The problem of the system of value emerged more acutely in later years and now seems to occupy Rickert's entire attention. By Rickert's work, both groups of problems have brought transcendental philosophy of value on to an epistemological foundation and organized it into a system. We must now become acquainted with the fundamental epistemological problem in Rickert's formulation. Thereby we direct attention to the continuity and development of philosophy of value. We see in what way Rickert takes up Windelband's (theoretical) investigations on theoretical philosophy, and further, how to the present day Rickert's epistemological work has developed under the decisive, but not purely adopted and elaborated, influence of quite differently oriented philosophical research.

[176] Proceeding from the distinction between judgement and evaluation as prompted by Brentano, Windelband's logical works concentrated on the problem of judgement. The essence of judgement lies in the alternate actions of affirmation and denial, approval and disapproval, acknowledgement and rejection. At the same time he indicates as a necessary task for all future logic the discovery of the – in Kant unsatisfactory – genuine connection between formal and epistemological logic, proceeding from the logical problems of judgement, concept and proof, to the epistemological questions. Rickert's work now sets off in this direction.

PART TWO

Critical Considerations [177]

§ 9. The Influence of Phenomenology on Rickert

Our critical considerations focus on the problem of the 'object of knowledge' and of the knowledge of the object, from whose solution the system of transcendental philosophy of value as a scientific worldview has to be constructed. This problem, which Rickert poses from the organic context of the previously indicated development of philosophy of value, has occupied him intensely from the beginning of his philosophical career until today. At the same time, his ever more detailed (not in the sense of special topics, but individual basic moments of its constitution) and more precise conceptions display changes that clearly reflect the influence of contemporary philosophical developments. The decisive refashionings are realized under the strong influence of Husserl's *Logical Investigations,* partly on direct paths, partly indirectly by way of Lask, who, proceeding from the insights of the *Logical Investigations* went further than Rickert, without, however, taking the step into phenomenology.

This influence of phenomenology is obscured particularly because its basic motives are not embraced, and because where they are named they are only polemicized against. I note these connections in principle and by way of introduction, not to cast doubt on [178] Rickert's originality, but in order to highlight the simple fact that the decisive insights of phenomenology cannot be avoided by the strange belief that these can be eclectically amalgamated to one's own standpoint without the latter becoming in its methodological fundamental structure an incomprehensible hybrid.

The development of Rickert's elaborations of the epistemological problem of the object occurs in the three editions of his book *The Object of Knowledge*, with which he qualified at this university in 1891. The first edition of this work appeared in 1892, comprising 91 small-format pages. The second edition appeared in 1904; in details it is more sharply formulated, the phenomenon of sense more precisely brought out and above all expanded through the appended treatment of the problem of categories. As is externally evident by its 456 large-format pages, the third edition of 1915 has become an entirely new book. Rickert says in the Foreword to this edition that 'previous editions should no longer be used'.[1] However, since the fundamental thought of the first edition is retained, I will concentrate on this first short characterization and on indicating the historical context of the problem in the first edition. Moreover, the decisive thoughts of Rickert come more sharply to expression here, not being so overburdened by broad and cumbersome critical controversies with unnamed opponents, which occur especially in the third edition.

Rickert's decisive developments lie between the second and third editions and are revealed in essays appearing in the interval, first in the [179] fundamental essay 'Two Ways of Epistemology'.[2] Like other writings to be mentioned, it is worked into the third edition, in part verbatim. Under the influence of the *Logical Investigations* Rickert came to see the necessity of adding a second way to the first. The essay is an unacknowledged confrontation with Husserl, at the same time taking over essential intuitions and thus the deficiencies which then still attached to them. Immediate stimulus from Kroner's 1908 dissertation *On Logical and Aesthetic Validity* and from Lask's 1909 lecture to the Philosophy Congress in Heidelberg, 'Is There a Primacy of Practical Reason in Logic?',[3] which basically repeats Husserl's 'critique of all normative logic' in the first volume of the *Logical Investigations*. From this new position there develops the series of *Logos* essays: 'On The Concept of Philosophy' (Vol. I, 1910); 'The One Unity and the Singular' (Vol. II, 1911–12), an unacknowledged discussion of Natorp's *Logical Foundations of the Exact Sciences* (1910) and the concept of number developed therein – here Rickert places the form-content problem in the foreground, anticipating the Laskian conception of judgement, known to him from personal conversations with Lask; 'Life-Values and Cultural Values' (Vol. II, 1911–12), a dispute with Bergson; 'Judgement and Judging', (Vol. III, 1912), nothing new; 'On the System of Values' (Vol. IV, 1913), a systematic programme of value-philosophy; and [180] 'On Logical and Ethical Validity' (*Kantstudien* XX, 1914).

Lask's two important systematic investigations appear in this period: *The Logic of Philosophy and the Doctrine of Categories: A Study of the Ruling Domain of Logical Form* (1911); and *The Doctrine of Judgement* (1912). Although Rickert did not follow the Laskian intuitions, he explicitly recognized the significance of the latter work for his own development, and expressed this by dedicating the third edition of *The Object of Knowledge* to Lask's memory. As the distinctive novelties of the third edition of *Object* Rickert mentions: 1) the emphasis on the value character of the logical or ideal as opposed to every ontology of the ideal; 2) the elaboration of the problem of knowledge as the problem of form; 3) the definitive refusal of all psychologism.[4]

Emil Lask, to whose investigations I personally owe very much, died in the battle at Galicia, in May 1915; his body was never found. He was one of the strongest philosophical personalities of our time, a serious man who in my view was on the way to phenomenology, whose writings are rich in ideas – however, they are not for casual readers.

I would like to preface the following critical considerations with a statement from Rickert himself, a statement which he sees as necessary at that place in his eulogy to Windelband where he takes a critical attitude to his own teacher: 'The *systematizer must at times be intolerant.*'[5]

The basic direction of my critical considerations was already laid down in critical reports which I gave in Rickert's 1913 seminar, when reviewing Lask's *Doctrine of Judgement*. I encountered great resistance there, [181] which, however, needless to say, in no way disrupted my personal relation to Rickert. The present low standing of what one could call 'scientific ethos' makes it necessary to say that even in the most radical struggle over the subject-matter personal relations remain undisturbed, because the scientific man must effect an absolute ἐποχή that brackets these out.

§ 10. Guiding Principles of the Critique

No critique just for its own sake. Positive aim, and not just a new theory of knowledge or a new epistemological 'standpoint'.

Idea of primordial science – scientific philosophy. *Basic critique* – of the method for the scientific determination of objects as such.

Method cannot be arbitrarily imposed on a region of objects, but in its structural content it develops in accordance with the aim of knowledge and the regional fundamental character of a determinate field of knowledge. It cannot be treated, therefore, as fully detached from the problem. It is a matter of understanding the latter in its main tendency and as it arises from historical motivation. Therefore the first edition, despite Rickert's remark. This is all the more permissible in that we do not subject it to critique, but through an examination of his development which at a turning-point begins with a consideration of method, we allow its critical rejection to be given by Rickert himself. The first edition, which despite the many considerations on the mode of object determination shows no *basic* methodological consciousness, will now be characterized expressly in relation to its general approach, its deficiencies highlighted and its relative legitimacy determined.

[182] For us the questions arise:

1) Is this methodological reflection radical?
2) Is there a genuine improvement in approach?
3) Do *those* results emerge that Rickert wants, and in which his knowledge is characteristically expressed?

The main defects of this absence of method show themselves in the failure to grasp a necessary side of the total problem – the *problem of the subject* – and above all by the fact that the second way, whose results are supposed to agree with those of the first, but are of still more dubious form, is also necessarily affected by them.

Kantian movement – problem of transcendence; Riehl, Schuppe, Volkelt, Dilthey, *Cremerius*.

'To the concept of knowledge there belongs, as well as a subject that knows, an object that is known.'

Being – consciousness; reality of the external world.

Principle of immanence: 'The Being of every reality must be regarded as a Being in consciousness.'[6]

Knowledge = representation. 'What then are representations supposed to portray and depict, if there is nothing outside the representations, if there is no original with which the copy agrees?'[7]

If knowledge is supposed to have meaning, we must presuppose that we grasp something independent of the theoretical subject.[8]

'What reasons do we have for thinking that knowledge copies a reality through representations, and that knowledge as such is to be found in *representations*?'[9]

Division of Being into things and representations; the latter as copy at a place. From 'the simplest epistemological considerations' [183] the intuition becomes problematic: '*problem of space*'! Thing and representation – *two objects* in the subject, which *establishes* their agreement.[10]

Aristotle: knowledge = judging. (Connecting representations? Nothing new obtained.)[11]

'Is it supposed to be possible to demonstrate the judgement as a process of autonomous significance?'

'For the present we see only what every individual confirms for himself.'
'We only want to know what happens when we judge.'[12]

'*Knowledge is affirmation or denial*. We want to discover the consequences of this.'[13]

'*Knowledge is recognition or rejection.*'

'Not through representations, but through affirmation or denial, can the knowing subject gain what it seeks with knowledge.'[14]

Feeling of evidence, a power announces itself in this, a power to which I am bound.

'We know nothing of a Being which we depict with representations. There is absolutely nothing to which our representation could be directed. On the other hand, when we want to judge, an ought provides immediate direction.'[15]

The problem of origin. Origin of method – origin of the object of primordial science and its primal structure. Our critical undertaking, which is itself phenomenology, encounters a difficulty because Rickert went through a development [184] determined precisely by phenomenological insights. Critical and rigorously methodological precision is needed to separate the genuine from the non-genuine, and genuine progress from errors.

§ 11. Rickert's Conception of the Fundamental Epistemological Problem. The Subjective Way

Knowledge cannot be representation, for there is no independent something towards which representations can direct themselves. If all Being is content of consciousness, how can there be an original which representations are supposed to copy?

Above all, so long as one regards knowledge as representation, an element which necessarily belongs to the concept of knowledge is not present: the knowing subject. For things like representations are objects, and the standpoint of knowledge as representation has to do not with a relation between subject and object, but with a relation between two objects, a relation which becomes quite incomprehensible as knowledge, for a subject is required that ascertains this copying of things by representations – and this knowledge cannot itself be a representation.

It was already known to Aristotle that truth 'is only contained in *judgements*'.[16] With this, however, little is gained so long as one thinks that what characterizes judgements is the connection or analysis of representations. For then it is again a matter of representations, and the old difficulties begin over again. The judgements too would have somehow to be directed to a transcendent Being 'in order to provide knowledge'.

[185] What if this concept of judgement were erroneous? 'Is it possible to exhibit judgement as a process of autonomous meaning?'[17] If the attempt must fail to find a *Being* independent of all *representations*, so the possibility is opened of finding something independent of the *judging* subject, so that it forms '*a standard for knowledge which reaches beyond the content of consciousness*'.[18]

a) Judgement and Value

The problem is now the judging subject. 'We only want to know what happens when we judge.' 'We see at the beginning only what every individual can confirm.' 'For us it is a matter of establishing what is *everywhere* present, where something is asserted as true, and therefore we can only be intent on a general concept of judgement which contains what is implicit in every item of knowledge, irrespective of what it treats.'[19]

Rickert considers it one of the 'most valuable insights of recent logical and phenomenological research' that to representations an 'element is added' which does not have the character of a representation. This '*factum*' is not sufficiently appreciated in its implications.[20]

Windelband gave 'the most transparent and . . . most comprehensive form' to this conception of judgement.[21] It is not possible to judge 'without affirming or denying'. 'Only through affirmation and denial [is] the representational relation [186] made into anything . . . to which the predicates true or untrue could apply.'[22] 'Knowing is acknowledging or rejecting.'[23] 'Knowing is affirming or denying. We want to try to discover the consequences.'[24] Rickert explicitly rejects the opinion of Brentano that the judgement, because it contains a non-representational element (affirmation and denial), is a different kind of relation between consciousness and object: 'For us, this assertion would presuppose too much.'[25] Rickert sees therein an unproven theory of the psychic. It could be that upon deeper analysis these questionable elements turn out to have the character of representation – indeed perhaps judgement is 'as psychic condition . . . nothing else but a complex of sensation'.[26]

What does process as psychic mean, and what does 'psychic process' mean? What is more laden with presuppositions and theory: if I say that I share *in* a content of consciousness and I consider *it* not only in a disengaged way, or if Brentano says that judgement and representation are different kinds of relation between consciousness and object? Rickert wants to distance himself from these theories, he wants 'simply to establish a fact'.[27] Thus he inquires about which species of psychic process judgement belongs to if a distinction is made between conditions 'in which we act with contemplative indifference' and conditions 'in which we take, or appear to take, an interest in the content of our consciousness as in something valuable'. Judgement does not amount to unengaged contemplation 'but it comes to expression in affirmation or denial, praise or blame'. Correct division of *psychic [187] processes*! 'Representation in the one class, and judgement, feeling and willing . . . in the other'. In the judgement a 'practical' comportment.[28]

'*Because what holds for judgement must also hold for knowledge*, it emerges . . . that theoretical knowledge too depends on a relationship to a value. Only in connection with values do the attitudes of praise or blame have any meaning. What I affirm must please me, what I deny must excite my disapproval. Knowing is therefore a process determined by feelings, i.e. by pleasure and displeasure.' Rickert himself admits that 'this may sound strange', but it is 'just the indubitable consequence' of his conception of judgement. Consequences are to be drawn from the establishment of facts (how often and by which subjects?). 'Feelings, therefore, are what guide our knowledge. The knowledge act itself can only consist in recognizing the value of feelings.'[29]

b) Evidence and Validity

Since it is apparent that only through affirmation or denial does the subject obtain what is sought in knowledge (affirmation or denial?), we need, in order to discover the object of knowledge, only to become familiar with this feeling. 'We have seen that in all knowledge a value is recognized. How do we distinguish this value from other feelings to which we relate in the mode of agreement? We speak here, initially, only of what we all do.'[30]

Through judgement we confirm a feeling of pleasure 'in which the drive to knowledge is stilled', and we call [188] this feeling 'certainty' (evidence). 'With every judgement I know, at the moment when I judge, that I recognize something *timeless*.' The evidence which, psychologically considered, is a feeling of displeasure, lends to the judgement a timeless validity and thus gives it a value. At the same time I experience myself *bound* by the feeling of evidence. I cannot arbitrarily affirm or deny. 'I feel myself determined by a power to which I subordinate myself and towards which I direct myself. The power is present with every judgement that I make . . . The one or the other judgement is always necessary.' The evidence, 'the feeling', gives 'the character of necessity' to the judgement.[31]

This necessity is not a causality of psychological mechanism: it is a necessity not of the must [*des Müssens*], but of the ought [*des Sollens*]. 'What leads my judgements, and thereby my knowledge, is the feeling that I *should* judge in such and such a way.' 'If we maintain only what we really know, we will have to admit the following. We know nothing of a Being which we copy with representations.' 'On the other hand, an ought immediately gives direction when we want to judge.' 'When I hear a sound, I am *forced* to judge that I hear a sound' – i.e. 'that with the sound an ought is given [if I want to judge!], an ought which demands and receives assent from a possible judgement'.[32]

Truth of judgement can only be defined with the help of a value 'which is to be recognized from the judgement'.[33] The value of judgements is not derivative; it applies to them not because they are true, but they are true in so far as a value is recognized in them. This applies to all judgements, thus to all assertions about reality. They are not true because they agree with reality, [189] because they assert what really is, but *real* is what is recognized by judgements. The real becomes a species of the true. The true judgement is the judgement that ought to be made. And why should the judgement be made? Because it is the true. Rickert wants to ascertain the existence of this circle. But this cannot satisfy those unable to free themselves from the old idea of knowledge as representation.

c) The Transcendence of the Ought

'One tries to find some other kind of ground for the truth of the judgement that I am now seeing letters of the alphabet, than the immediate feeling of the ought, the necessity *so* to judge.'[34] What is the object of knowledge? If we designate as object that which knowledge, i.e. judgement, is directed towards, then the object which is recognized in the judgement can only be the ought. This standard fully suffices for knowledge. '*We cannot discover anything else* except the order of the content of consciousness, i.e. the relations between representations which should pertain and are therefore to be affirmed.'[35]

Is this ought really, in every respect, an independent transcendent object of knowledge? What is announced – in the judgemental necessity, in the evidence – is a feeling. Can one ascribe to a feeling anything more than subjective significance? How is this transcendence of the ought to be grounded? By showing that the denial of the ought leads to contradictions. In this way the legitimacy of accepting this transcendence is shown. 'Why should the ought be recognized?' Does it lend to knowledge the sought-after 'objectivity' ? Until now we know only: 'If [190] there is an object of knowledge at all, this is to be found only in the ought, not in Being.'[36]

The denial of a transcendent Being can never lead to contradictions. For all judgements that appear to relate to transcendent Being can be reformulated in such a way that they only assert facts of consciousness. Instead of 'The sun shines' I can say 'I see the sun'. In this way a transcendent Being no longer comes into question. Is it now possible to reformulate the judgement in such a way that it no longer contains acknowledgment of an ought independent of a subject? 'Clearly not, for we have shown that *every* judgement consists in the acknowledgment of judgemental *necessity,* and this necessity always implies an ought from which the knowing subject is independent.'[37] One can change around judgements in whatever way, one will always have to acknowledge their truth-value as a fully independent transcendent value. So long as I actually judge, the transcendent ought is always acknowledged and is therefore also absolutely indubitable. Every denial of the ought cancels itself out, for every denial is a judgement, and as such acknowledgement of a transcendent ought.

To 'prove' this transcendence would not have required the whole book, for it has nothing to do with what is being discussed!! Rickert shows only that in knowledge *something or other* is acknowledged (should be truth). The constitution of all Being in *meaning* is not thereby demonstrated.

The ought is therefore conceptually prior to Being. 'All our expositions rest on the two propositions that judgement is not representation, and that "Being" only has meaning as component part of a judgement.'[38] 'We wanted only to prove the transcendent "minimum", which everyone acknowledges [191] however he might otherwise think about knowledge.'[39] What are the methodological presuppositions here? Expositions in relation to the sphere of experience, indeed about *reality* and *intentionality*.

In a certain, albeit methodologically quite inadequate, way, Rickert has achieved this. He has shown that every act of acknowledgement is somehow motivated, that it stands in a motivational totality. This is not shown with methodological rigour; he *wanted* to show this. However, it is a great error when Rickert thoroughly hypostasizes this motive character to the *object* of knowledge and thereby believes himself to have solved the transcendental problem of constitution! For it is not made clear what 'object' is supposed to mean, nor what it means to 'be directed' towards this. Further: this 'transcendental minimum' can be found in every experience and as such is in no way suitable for characterizing the theoretical relation. To show this would not have required all these deliberations, but simply what Rickert still lacks, namely clear insight into the methodological problem of research into experience.

Is this now recognized in the methodological considerations of the 'two ways', and in the second edition of *Object*? How does Rickert characterize the methodological character of his reflections? I leave out of account that Rickert's current interpretation of his procedures draws in problems and perspectives that were worked out by Husserl.[40]

§ 12. The Transcendental-Logical (Objective) Way as the Method of Grounding the Presuppositions of the Subjective Way [192]

We have arrived at a decisive point in our considerations. Rickert shows basic deficiencies in the subjective way and its need of supplementation by a second way. The subjective way 'does not let the *grounding* emerge, which, if its results hold, is actually decisive for them'.[41] It must be demonstrated that real knowledge directs itself at a value. If that is proven (Rickert *wants* to show that) then the subjective way has a secure foundation and can unreservedly take its entitlements and show its *basic superiority*, for ultimately it is the defining methodology of transcendental philosophy. As Rickert says himself: 'Without taking account of real knowledge and its immanent meaning transcendental philosophy would remain quite empty.'[42]

But besides the decisive grounding of the subjective way, of the authentic method of transcendental philosophy, the objective way achieves something else of basic significance. By demonstrating the valuational character of the theoretical it forces us, scientifically, 'to acknowledge the region of theoretical meaning as a *region of value*',[43] i.e. logic (theoretical philosophy) is science of value and so too is all of *philosophy*. A vast region of specific investigations opens up for logic as 'pure doctrine of value', a region distinct from all ontology. Logic has nothing to do with Being, but is concerned with formations of value. Thus opposition to all logic as purported science of Being, as conceived by Bolzano and by the philosopher who most profoundly built upon [193] Bolzano's ideas, i.e. Husserl.

With the proof of the valuational character of truth, therefore, the objective way has to provide the ultimate foundation of philosophy *as* science of value.

First we follow the objective way and see if it provides the foundation for the subjective. If truth is a *value*, then I can come to a transcendence, to an ought, to acknowledgement, I can show that acts of judgement, if they are to contain *knowledge*, must mean rejection or acknowledgement. In short, it is then proved that knowledge is valuing [*Werten*] and not looking [*Schauen*].

I note here that Rickert is in error if he thinks that the only presupposition of the 'constructive' method of interpretation is that the relation to value *must* be acknowledgement if it is shown that possible comportment to values *can* be *acknowledgement*. It must *then* be so, if it is to achieve something for knowledge. What does knowledge mean here? Acknowledgement? Or something else! Knowledge – of what? Of values.

To be noted: nothing is permitted to be ascertained; a Being is simply *valued*. We have to ask how this Being is objective, what Rickert intends with this psychic Being. It would have to be shown that I can comport to

145

values only by way of acknowledgement or rejection, or: that there are several possible ways of comporting.

We focus on two things:

1) Is the value-character of truth proved by Rickert?
2) If this is proved, does it follow that logic is doctrine of value, that philosophy is essentially science of value?

Rickert demonstrates neither the one nor the other, indeed he has not even seen the problem of value at all. This, therefore, is the ultimate sense of philosophy of value!!

[194] How does the objective way proceed? Clearly, as Rickert says himself, it may not proceed via the detour of transcendental philosophy. It is supposed precisely to overcome the latter's difficulties, which consist in: 1) that it must *pre*suppose something which is ungrounded, 2) that it must proceed from a fact or psychic Being from which 'nothing *determinately* transcendent can be extracted',[44] in particular not what Rickert wishes to and must extract in order to maintain the theory. Nothing *determinate*, but in the end still *something*; then the interpretation would be in the decisive point unnecessary. And what does it mean: an indeterminate transcendent can be 'extracted'?

Nothing can be obtained by just ascertaining facts, but only by interpreting the psychic Being, i.e. by 'putting something *into*' what is ascertained. Clearly, the objective method cannot proceed in this way. But it also must 'attach to a generally known *fact*'. In this respect it is not different from the subjective way. And this, i.e. that epistemology must connect with 'facts', does not further disturb Rickert.[45]

The problem is not connection with a fact, but that the subjective way must connect with the act as psychical being (*empirical reality*), from which and at which nothing else can be obtained by ascertaining facts than just psychical Being and moments of Being.

If therefore the objective way too must connect up with a fact, we ask: What is *this reality* from which epistemology discovers the object of knowledge? Its problem is the knowledge of truth. I must therefore *proceed* from a reality to which truth is attached, and which for this reason may also be called true. [195] Are the acts the only realities which 'in this sense [that truth attaches to them] may be called true' ? Does truth attach to a psychical Being of acts as to the Being of word complexes? No. 'We hear a number of words, or we read them. In their totality they form a *sentence*.'[46] I say: 'But Kaiser transfinite neither not which triangle died if.' A cluster of words – do they form in their totality a sentence? Rickert will answer: only a cluster of words which expresses a *true judgement* is a genuine sentence and a *true* sentence. To be sure, Rickert admits that I must *understand* the words, their meanings, I must understand what the sentence *expresses* in order to say it is true. Therefore a sentence is true only in so far as it *is understood*. It is not a matter of sounds and signs, of acoustical and optical data, but of acts of understanding and intending. Therefore, if Rickert wants to be consistent, we are in the old position: with psychic acts, with a Being from which we cannot extract anything without putting something in and interpreting it. How does Rickert know from the objective way anything about acts of understanding and intending, whose accomplishment consists in understanding and intending something? From where has he suddenly interpreted them, when it is really a matter of avoiding the deficiencies of the subjective way and of first securing the foundation of all meaning interpretation through the objective way? But, Rickert concedes, 'The acts as psychic acts are no more true than the sentence as word-complex. What is properly true is only what is meant as true or is understood',[47] the *content of the judgement*. Thus, in the experience of the judgement, other *acts* are apparently essential!

[196] Rickert suddenly knows of something intended, something understood, a *judgemental content*. Clearly the content does not attach to the sound complex, but emerges only in an intentional act. But from a psychic Being I cannot extract anything, the subjective way failed at this. Indeed I cannot even say that an act is one of acknowledgment if I do not first put this meaning into psychical Being. Rickert comes to something transcendent neither from the fact of the psychic Being of acts, nor from the fact of word complexes. He is not permitted, and does not want, to enact the interpretation of meaning. What remains? He ascertains 'that, whereto the psychic act directs itself or its content'.[48] Suddenly the act is no longer psychic Being, but directs itself to something; it has a content. Suddenly something can be extracted – and it is unclear why that should not already be possible through the subjective way. I need only do what Rickert suddenly does through the so-called objective way: free myself from theory, not constructively elevating a fiction to a method, but taking the act as it is, namely in its directedness at something, and, as Rickert says himself, 'directly look at' this 'something'.[49]

Therefore I either grasp the acts directly in the way they give themselves, ascertaining what they direct themselves to – likewise the character of being directed towards, as Rickert does through the so-called objective way – or I grasp the acts as psychic Being or word complex as facts, in which case one would never come to anything like the content of acts. The construction of meaning interpretation is no help, for this would have meaning, if at all, only from content. Also not through the objective way. The *basic superiority* of the subjective way rests [197] on a pure fiction, a fiction from which, ultimately, a method of epistemology is made wherein one must not admit what one does. His two ways are simply construction.

The second way differs from the first in that Rickert, under the compulsion of the facts, 'directly apprehends' the acts and their content, thereby freeing himself from the constructive assumptions of the first way. There is only one way of epistemology, which offers various possible perspectives.

That Rickert himself has to admit that the objective way also needs acts is seen in his statement: 'If psychic acts of intending and understanding necessarily occur in the epistemologist, he can push these aside as inessential, and immediately turn to the theoretical content.'[50]

To this is simply to be remarked that in the epistemologist, i.e. in his methodological attitude, psychic Being should *never* occur, and that therefore it does not need to be pushed aside. But the acts in their phenomenal experiential character are certainly there and may never be pushed aside as inessential, also not when I undertake genuine analysis of content.

This objective judgemental content, *which as such was ascertained*, 'I will therefore investigate, in order to find the object of knowledge'.[51] Since this content remains independent of psychic act, it can be called transcendent meaning. Rickert indicates that this meaning is neither physical nor psychical, but presents the 'ideal' content of the statement.

We know: the content is different from the act, and in a particular way, not only in the case of perception, where act and content belong to the real content of consciousness, [198] to immanent Being (processes). Notice the quite distorted illustration of perception, perceptual content. The transcendental meaning *is* something '*unreal*'.[52]

Therefore the further question is: what is this meaning in its unity, this meaning which we understand in a true sentence? Rickert explicitly emphasizes (what has long been known) that the meaning of a sentence is a specific unity and may not be torn apart into individual meanings; these in themselves are never true, and therefore one cannot study the problem of truth through them! Rickert does not see that this study, if it is to be scientifically fruitful, in principle presupposes another. Certainly – but the 'objective way'. Rickert sees its advantage in that it departs immediately from the 'sentence', whereby nothing is said about what 'sentence' is: thus the sentence must be understood; and indeed is so only in that every word and then the unitary meaning of the words are understood. That is, a scientific philosophy will see that there are problems of principle here which underpin everything else, which one cannot dismiss with common ways of speaking about word, meaning, sentence and significance. Then one will be prevented from 'philosophizing' from a great height about transcendent meaning, as Rickert goes on to do.

Should meaning be in any way attributed to beings or existing things? What the existing thing is, is given by its Being; this is nowhere clarified. Does it belong to the ideal being of mathematical forms? No. If one wanted to bring together meaning and ideal Being, one could say at best that 'the individual word meanings which contain the sense lie in the sphere of ideal sense'.[53] But 'we know' (until now a bare assertion) that meaning is never grasped just by joining together simple word meanings. [199] There is still lacking an essential element of the meaning, which constitutes its unity and upon which its transcendence rests – the *truth*. This will therefore have to be more closely considered, especially with respect to how it constitutes the unity of meaning upon which its transcendence rests. (Unity of meaning, that which constitutes it, and transcendence of meaning, are in no way identical.) Meaning, therefore, cannot be conceived as something existing, an entity, and be accommodated in the sphere of Being, unless one wants to indifferently designate everything whatsoever which is thinkable as Being, in which case meaning is also a Being. (Question meaning – no unity; and question yet theoretically indifferent, neither value nor non-value.) 'Meaning lies ... "before" all beings and cannot be grasped by any ontology.'[54] How therefore? Now comes the great discovery and the proof!

In order correctly to assess the new element that now comes into consideration, it is necessary to summarize what Rickert has previously established concerning the transcendent meaning. Departing from a true sentence, he has established that such a thing does indeed exist. A sentence is true only in so far as it contains a true meaning. This true meaning is different from the acts, it is *unreal*, it maintains itself timelessly, it is valid, as one reformulates being-true when one wants to avoid the expression 'being'.

Let us recall what is supposed to be gained through the objective way: the grounding of the presuppositions of the subjective way – 'If we are permitted to assume that truth is a value'.

We must not incorporate meaning within the sphere of existing entities. To what sphere is it to be referred? We are confronted by a fundamental problem, by reference to which the basic character of logic (of theoretical philosophy) and of philosophy in general is to be decided.

[200] But we will not continue in the previous manner, looking still more closely at what I 'directly apprehend' and showing its determinations, but it must be proved – with a real method. I circle around the matter, do not directly look at it, and see if I thus discover something about it. (It would not be a method if I simply ascertain what it is in itself, for I have established it, directly looked at it – it, the meaning itself, as has been said, is no psychical Being, etc.)

Rickert does *not* look at the judgemental content. He does not *observe* according to the purported valuational character of meaning. He circles around the meaning! And on this way, in which I cannot see the meaning, he seeks a *criterion*, on the basis of which I can decide whether what is present is a concept of Being or of value. Nothing more precise. (Various things can be intended.) Rickert decides whether an existing entity, or something valid with the character of value, is present.

This criterion consists in *negation*! Negation is a concept of Being: thus the contrast is unambiguous. Negation is a pure value concept: thus the contrast is ambiguous (either nothing or a non-value). So by virtue of ambiguous or unambiguous negation, I know whether it is something or a value concept. Applied to the transcendent, meaning negates: 1) nothing; 2) false or untrue meaning. Therefore meaning is a value. Is this *criterion of negation* genuine?[55]

Rickert does not bother to ask about my right to use this phenomenon as a criterion. How do I know that it is valid?

§ 13. Considerations on Negation [201]

Negation of something. Negation: *formal* function within the region of objectivity. Negation has no determinate regional character, but applies to everything whatsoever. From negation as such there is never determined the *negative* in its what and regional character, but always only from the what of *that which* is negated, and the how of regional oppositions is first determined from this. Oppositions, which express themselves in negation, can therefore be characterized only as *regional*, not through the formal Not.

Essentially (*a priori*) impossible that simple negation is the criterion for regional characterization.

Three types of opposition are to be distinguished:

1) formal-ontological opposition (something in general – nothing)
2) regional opposition (empirical being – ideal being)
3) internal regional opposition (warm–cold; straight–crooked) (regionally characterized; with these according to essential aspects).

The statements hold:

1) Every regional and internal regional opposition can be formalized (to the negation of the something in general) and has as its opposition the *Nothing*.
2) With the concretion of objective characteristics grows the number of possibilities of opposition.

With his criterion, Rickert has not only not demonstrated the meaning of value, he *a priori* cannot do this. But we have not thereby grasped the problem at a sufficiently basic level.

Rickert wants to classify meaning within a particular region, and indeed this classification is of the greatest significance: it decides the total character of philosophy. If this classification is to be accomplished in a scientific-methodological manner and absolutely grounded, then a preliminary [202] matter needs to be dealt with: the characterization of region and demarcation in general, the difficult problem of 'fulfilment' and the further problem of how this is to be carried out, what do I inquire into, what are the *a priori* possibilities for characterizing regions?[56]

By claiming that it is no more possible to define Being than it is to define value, nothing is actually said. At most this indicates that one has not yet seen the difficult problems here, or that philosophy does not give definitions in the usual sense.

Value: 'For structures which do not exist and yet are something.' How does Rickert know that such a thing exists? But I have indeed shown this;

therefore the structure is a value. Why therefore the cumbersome and confusing business about a criterion?

Rickert is much too philosophical to be content with this, i.e. he admits implicitly that nothing is achieved with the definition of value.

What is the problem?

Location of true judgemental meaning in the sphere of value. The three forms of opposition. Notice the third, as it is present. There are internal regional oppositions, which are characterized regionally. If therefore, according to Rickert, warm and cold are opposed to one another, the objection is decisive only when a contrast of meaning is supposed to be present; but that cannot mean it is the same opposition as *true and false*.

When Rickert protests against this, he is quite correct. Whether it is *an object of value* – or an object of a quite distinctive region – remains problematic. Doubtless there is an analogy with objects of value; perhaps it is itself a value-opposition – that I do not venture to decide, for that philosophy is by a long way insufficient (in principle).

[203] I remarked earlier that a basic failing of the book is that Rickert restricts himself to positive judgement. Let us take a negative one, in order to see what ambiguity actually disturbs Rickert. 'This triangle is not heavy' is a negative judgement, i.e. if positive means true, negative false. These two opposites 'positive–negative' are quite differently situated in the meaning of the judgement. Positive – as *ascribing a predicate* – belongs to the *structural characteristic* of judgemental meaning as such, and positive – as *true* – is not a structural characteristic, but itself a *predicate*, which is ascribed in a positive way.

If what is meant is positive as positive value, then the problem is whether true and false may be characterized as positive and negative value. *If I assume this*, if I take true as positive in value, then *negation* is not only a negative as such, but at the same time *negative* in the sense of non-valuable.

Rickert confuses this ambiguity *with the first*. It is not that negation is ambiguous as *negating*, but the word negation has different meanings where I bring a value-opposition into relation with the judgemental structure. But whether there is such an opposition is precisely the problem. In other words: Rickert speaks of a twofold ambiguity: ambiguous = two opposites – at the same time: ambiguous = two meanings of negative.

APPENDIX I
On the Nature of the University and Academic Study
Summer Semester 1919

(Transcript by Oskar Becker)

Situation in the life-context: a situation is a certain unity in natural experience [*Erlebnis*]. Situations can interpenetrate one another: their durations do not exclude each other (e.g. a year in the field, a semester: no objective concept of time). In every situation a unitary tendency is present. It contains no static moments, but 'events'. The occurrence of the situation is not a 'process' – as could be theoretically observed in the physical laboratory, e.g. an electrical discharge. Events 'happen to me'. The basic form of the life-context is *motivation*. In situational experiences it recedes. The motivating and the motivated are not given explicitly. They pass implicitly through the 'I'. The intentionality of all experiences of a situation has a definite character, which originates from the total situation. Example of a situation: 'going to the seminar'.

Dissolution of the situational character: this means the dissolution of the closedness of the situation, i.e. the aspect-determination, at the same time the dissolution of the situational 'I' and its tendential character. In this way an experiential emptiness occurs. The dissolution relates to the whole sphere of experience. There is a relationlessness between the things of a situation, i.e. no relationlessness of *meaning* (e.g. the objects on my writing desk constitute a situation).

[206] For example, climbing a mountain in order to see the sunrise. One has arrived at the top, and everyone experiences silently. One is totally given over to the event, one sees the sun's disc, the clouds, a mass of rocks of this definite form, but *not* as the specific mass that I have just

climbed. Here at any rate the I remains. On the other hand, no purely theoretical objectivity is possible. The objects are no longer held together by the situation; they are isolated. But a new different type of totality is constituted through the *meaning* of objective orientation.

Further on 'situation' : 1) Every situation is an 'event' and not a 'process'. What happens has a relation to me; it radiates into my own I. 2) The situation has a relative closedness. 3) Indistinguishability of the I in the situation. The I does not need to be in view, it flows with the situation.

Tendential character of experiences in the situation. Tendencies that are determined from the I. Every situation has its aspect from this tendency.

Every situation has 'duration'. The individual 'durations' of various situations *interpenetrate* each other (in the motivated and motivating). The I is itself a situational I; the I is 'historical'.

More precisely on the dissolution of the situational context: the situational character disappears. The unity of the situation is exploded. The experiences that do not possess any unity of meaning, substantive unity, lose the unity which the situation gave to them.

At the same time the situational I, the 'historical' I, is *suppressed*. There occurs the 'de-historicization of the I'. Prevention of the living relation of the I to its situation. The life-relation of the situational I is no simple directedness toward mere objects. Every experience is intentional, it [207] contains a 'view toward' something or other (a pure loving apprehending expecting remembering view). The 'view' has a 'quality' (quality of the act's character).

Now the modification toward the theoretical attitude can take place, i.e. every experience can deteriorate into 'mere directedness to'; it bears the possibility of dissolution and impoverishment within itself. The extent of this modification is unlimited, it governs all pure experiences.

There are only two basic types of this modification of the experiencing attitude into the theoretical attitude:

1) Maximum of theoretization. Greatest possible extinction of the situation.
2) Minimum of theoretization. Greatest possible maintenance of the situation.

To 1: View of natural science. What is experienced of nature is not only disengaged from the situational I, but is further theoreticized. The levels are: biological description – physical-mathematical theory (e.g. colours –

movements of the ether). Process of removal from the qualitatively given colour. Pinnacle: mathematical natural science. Mechanics, abstract electrodynamics, etc.

To 2: Consideration of history of art. The art historian is also confronted by objects. But they still bear in themselves the patina of passage through the historical I. The artwork is given as artwork, the character of experience is retained.

History of Religion: the historian of religion is concerned with Jesus as he is experienced by the pious. The figure of Jesus remains preserved as a religious figure. Here therefore we have a minimum of theoretization.

Both groups lead to two different types of science:

Type 1: sciences of explanation.
Type 2: sciences of understanding.

[208] With the second type the basic problem is: how is theoretization united with the unfolding of the experiential context?

The intuitive, inductive phenomenology, the philosophical primordial science, is a science of understanding.

The situational I: the I-self, the 'historical I', is a function of 'life-experience'. Life-experience is a continually changing context of situations, of motivational possibilities. Life-experience in the pure environing world is a mixed structure. Nevertheless it can be quite definitely described in its structure. Moreover there are genuine life-experiences, which grow out of a genuine life-world (artist, religious person).

Depending upon the genuine motivational possibilities, there arises the phenomenon of life-intensification (in the opposite case, minimizing of life). This phenomenon is not determined by a feeling of experienced content. There are people who have experienced much in various 'worlds' (artistically etc.) and yet are 'inwardly empty'. They have reached only a 'superficial' experience of life. Today the forms of life-intensification are becoming ever more pregnant, fraught with meaning. 'Activism' is in motive genuine, in form misguided. The 'free German youth movement' is in form genuine, but without fertility in its setting of goals.

To the formation of the experiential character accompanying the objectivities of the theoretical sphere belongs a characteristic inter-wovenness of the historical I and the theoretical I, along with the typical differences in cases 1 and 2.

Two types of *experiencedness* [*Erlebtheit*]: 1) lived *experiences* [*gelebte Erlebnisse*] as such; 2) experienced *contents*, that *which* I have experienced.

The form of context of each type of experience is different. The unity of E(2) is objective, a kind of situation, something with content. The unity of E(1) is the historical I, life-experience. The situations interpenetrate each other. [209] What is lived is dependent on motives that are functionally dependent on the past. The historical I is first shaped by the contexture of experience.

When an experiential situation is extinguished, that which is lived loses its situational, experiential unity. The contents fall apart, they are not an empty something, but they are dissolved out of the specific unity of the situation. The content as such externalizes itself from the situation, but still bears the character of externalization. The contents are something, but not simply formal objectivity. The 'something' of experienceability is to be distinguished from the formal something and is un-theoretical in nature.

With the dissolution of the situational context the experienced things keep the fullness of their content, but they stand there simply as states of affairs. The externalized sphere of experienced things is thereby defined. It is defined in its what, it is the 'one' and not the 'other'. This 'heterothesis' of the 'one' and of the 'other' is not to be understood in purely logical terms, but from the contexture of consciousness. This state of affairs of all that is experienced has in itself ('analytically') the possibility of further determination and in contrast to the other. The state of affairs implies a continuation, a reference away from itself. Every state of affairs refers to another. Such factual contextures have the character of a specific unity, i.e. one cannot continue in just any direction, but only within a certain region; from every state of affairs one comes to a 'natural boundary' : e.g. one cannot come to a religious problem from a mathematical state of affairs (cf. also Wölfflin, *Fundamental Concepts of Art History* [*Kunsthistorische Grundbegriffe*]; there Wölfflin starts out from the sphere of aesthetic states of affairs). From this unity of the factual contexture there arises a typology of states of affairs.

Everything experienced is something lived, something externalized, which makes it necessary to understand the externalized utterance itself; one must preserve the situational character. [210] That happens mostly in philosophy.

The modification to theoretical comportment is a modification to a new situation.

It is important that theoretical comportment be drawn in a teleologically necessary way into a material contexture. Theoretical comportment simply has states of affairs before itself. In so far as states of affairs bear a teleology within themselves, the theoretical comportment itself becomes a process. The experiential character of theoretical comportment is a progression from one factual determination to another. Every state of affairs is in its own terms a problem (πρόβλημα), something set and given [Aufgegebenheit]. There is a necessity of lawfulness in the progression. It marks the direction of the process of theoretical comportment. The direction is *method* (μέθοδος), the *way* to the constitution of the contexture of states of affairs. In so far as the theoretical comportment is necessary, yet still a problem, it finds its lawful progression in method.

We will now examine the modification no longer as modification *to* something, but *from* something (i.e. we will look backwards). The contexture of life-experience is a context of situations which interpenetrate each other. The fundamental character of life-experience is given through the necessary relation to *corporeality*. That is of fundamental significance. 'Sensibility' [*Sinnlichkeit*] (in *Plato* and *German idealism*) is life-experience.

The practical-historical I is necessarily of a *social* nature, it stands in the life-contexture with other I's. In all genuine life-worlds a connection always remains with 'natural life-experience'. The genesis of the fundamental level of the theoretical is conditioned through this.

Theoretical comportment requires constant renewal. Theoretical objectivity is accessible only through an ever new fresh impetus. This necessity of renewal [211] of genesis can be taken into a tendency. That means: this experience can be taken to the core of a new situation, thereby defining a situational contexture, a life-contexture as such.

The kind of genesis differs according to the theoretical objectivity (e.g. it is different for a mathematician and an art historian).

Aside from this difference, the genesis can still be differently realized.

In this respect we distinguish three types:

1) mere cognizance;
2) cognition (methodological solution);
3) cognitive discovery (research).

Comportment to the theoretical is not yet theoretical comportment.

Character of the state of affairs gives the character of the state of affairs as a problem, from this the idea of method in the relationship of the state of affairs to the subject.

The modification is itself *from* immediate life. In the life-stream a basic level: *corporeality* with the function of release of definite modificational contextures: 'sensibility'. Every experience is 'burdened' with this basic level, but there are forms of freeing and re-forming. *Francis of Assisi*: every natural life-experience is dissolved into a new meaning and with religious men can be understood only from there.

Theoretical comportment, in so far as it is directed in a comprehensive way toward pure states of affairs in which every emotional relation is strictly disallowed, removes itself from life-experience. The theoretical man necessarily tears himself away from the natural attitude. The theoretical world is not always there, but is accessible only in a constantly renewed divesting of the natural world.

[212] Theoretical comportment is a process first because it flows through a chain of grounding, but second because it tears itself from the contexture of life with ever novel spontaneity. Therefore tearing free and insertion within the teleology of connections of states of affairs. If theoretical comportment is taken in a tendency (when one poses to oneself the task of knowing a definite region), a *new situation* thereby results. We have therefore a new situational development. In this way a life-contexture oriented to the theoretical becomes possible.

The three types: cognizance [*Kenntnisnahme*], cognition [*Erkenntnisnahme*], research, are connected not only because the first calls for the second and the second for the third, but also because the third phase refers back to the first two in a clarifying way. Functional types, because they can be effective in various regions of being. All types together give a totality of scientific life. Task of investigation: the various levels of intensity of the types in a personality.

First Phase: cognizance: preliminary phase (preliminary form of the theoretical). It does not move beyond natural life-experience. The natural situation is not disturbed. The states of affairs are in this character (as such) not present in the cognizance; the what [*das Was*] is there in its simply being thus and so [*Sosein*].

Various levels of clarity and phases of cognizance (various goal-settings). Most people never go beyond simple cognizance. It can become a primal form only in the religious. Cognizance is characterized as a serene dedication to the *subject-matter*. It moves first of all in the regions of natural experience. These are of interest only in their being thus and so [*Sosein*]. Yet it is directed toward a particular contexture. ('Nature' in the 'nature-lore' of the elementary school.) This unity itself is not apprehended as such. *Education for truthfulness*.

[213] *New phase*: a habitus awakens in the knowing subject who is ready to go over to a new type, that of cognition.

Cognizance operates in new worlds: history and nature. New regions of subject-matter emerge in the form of unity. Particular forms of contexture emerge. With intensified sensitivity for differences the necessity for implanting absolute veracity always increases.

New comportment: cognizing *inquiry* concerning the possible modes and the apprehension of the contexture. A disposition is thereby created, such that wanting cognizance is transformed into wanting to know. Presentiment of a new world with new content. New possible comportment to this new world. Thereby the highest phase of education for cognizance is reached. Decisive is the absolute dedication to the matter, veracity. Necessity of a new obligation.

2nd Phase: cognition: pure dedication to the subject-matter. Situational content of the study: every life-relation is suppressed. I am fully free of every life-contexture and yet fully bound to the truth. To another subject I simply have the obligation of absolute veracity.

By entering into this pure sphere of states of affairs I obtain the chance of unlimited knowledge. But I assume the risk that, if I infringe against the condition of this life-contexture, I must withdraw from the scientific life-contexture. Therefore the 'vocational question' stands at the entrance to the theoretical life-contexture: can I maintain in myself the disposition to absolute veracity? The theoretical sphere is the sphere of absolute *freedom*, I am obligated only to the idea of scientificity. All other comportment must be guided *by this*. Not to use the other in any circumstances. I have only pure states of affairs [214] and their horizons. They must stem from the character of the region. Method is no artifice, but is conditioned by the matter and always originates anew.

Return to the *genesis of theoretical comportment*. The development of consciousness toward theoretical experience is fraught with three labilities.

1) *Lability in respect of the environmental experience*. Demand of the 'eternal youth' of the theoretical man. An ever new return to the origin, first spontaneity. Therefore a wavering between environmental and theoretical life, and a suffering under their opposition.

2) Danger of *splitting off from other experiential worlds* (art, religion, politics, etc.). This opposition between experiential worlds already begins at the level of cognizance; it must be 'closed down', 'brought to a halt'.

3) *Opposition between cognitive and investigative consciousness*, between the higher receptivity and the productivity. *Critical consciousness*: what is handed down loses the character of tradition, it must now be experienced; genuine questioning.

These labilities are necessary. They must not be avoided through method.

C. H. Becker, *Thoughts on University Reform* [*Gedanken zur Hochschulreform*], Leipzig 1919.

Worldview consists in being convinced. It sees a rank order. It grows from a particular life-world and sets out the rank-order of life-regions from there. It is not a scientific comportment.

APPENDIX II

The Idea of Philosophy and the Problem of Worldview

War Emergency Semester 1919

(Excerpt from the transcript by Franz-Josef Brecht)

8.IV.19

(Fundamental stance of phenomenology only attainable as a life-stance, through life itself.)

Object as the unity of a multiplicity, constituted through the unity of the laws of thought: according to Natorp this is the fundamental equivalence, the primal sense of consciousness.

In fact, however, Natorp's method of subjectivization is only an extension of the method of objectivization. Reconstruction is also construction. The objectivizing comportment. Apart from this, Natorp encounters difficulties that do not arise in the objectivizing method of the sciences. If, as Natorp maintains, there are no unmediated experiences, how can I employ immediacy as a criterion for genuine reconstruction? Reconstruction must presuppose a standard of judgement, but this can only be immediacy.

Natorp does *not* see the danger of psychologism in subjectivization. On his view psychology is the *logic* of the psychical. In the Marburg school, the theoretical-logical has the determining position. Every kind of knowledge is reduced to logic. (Renewal of Hegelian dialectic.) The logic of objects! Panarchy of the logos in the logical sense.

[216] To understand the opposition between Natorp's psychological and Husserl's phenomenological method, this idea of the absolutization of the logical should be kept firmly in mind.

So does description contain no theoretical encroachment of the immediate?

161

The insight, that Natorp does not see the sphere of experience in its primordial givenness.

Doing away with standpoints. Phenomenology is the philosophy without standpoints!

The principle of principles pertaining to the phenomenological attitude: everything given in primordial intuition is to be accepted just as it gives itself. No theory as such can change anything here, for the principle of principles is itself no longer theoretical; it expresses the fundamental life-stance of phenomenology: the sympathy of experience with life! This is the basic intention. It has nothing to do with irrationalism or the philosophy of feeling. Rather, this fundamental stance is itself clear, like life itself at its basic level. The fundamental phenomenological stance is not a routine – it cannot be mechanically acquired, which would make phenomenology a farce. It is nothing readily at hand, but must be slowly and strenuously acquired.

This phenomenological intuition – is it not itself a comportment to *something*? Separation of the originary given from theoretical reflection. Thus unavoidable objectivization of the originary given. Therefore indeed theoretical?

Fundamental difficulty: description, i.e. linguistic formulation, is supposed to be theoretically contaminated. This is because meaning is essentially such as to intend something *objectively*. It is the essence of meaning fulfilment to take an object as *object*. Further, the universality of word meaning must necessarily have the character of generalization, thus of theoretization. Intuitive comportment is identified with description itself, as if the method of [217] description were in the end a kind of intuition: I can indeed only describe what I have already seen.

But in intuition there is *something*. Thus intuition too contains a separation between the given and consciousness. Here is the *decisive* question, whether this is not itself a theoretical prejudice.

In the intuitive comportment I am looking at *something* [*etwas*]. The 'mere something' – the definiteness of objectivity in general is the most far removed from life, the highest point of de-vivification in the process of theorizing. Therefore indeed theoretical.

To see clearly, fundamental separation. Is the 'something in general' really the highest point of the de-vivification process, the absolute theoretization? It can be shown that this *prejudice* is theoretical.

To see this: the experience of the lectern. Process of progressive theoretization: in the end 'the elements are something' .

It emerges that the characterization 'it is something' can be directed at *every level* of the process of objectivization.

From this emerges the principle that the individual stages in the process of de-vivification are subject to a specific graduation; by contrast the form of objectivity 'something in general' is *free, not* tied to stages.

It is therefore evident that formal objectivity does not at all belong here, further that the 'something in general' is not theoretically motivated at all.

11. IV. 19

It is necessary to see the fundamental necessity for phenomenology: that the 'something in general' does not belong in the de-vivification process of theoretization, but rather in the primal phenomenological sphere.

[218] Environmental experience: *stages* of objectivization and progressive de-vivification; each possessing a founding motive and qualitative character as a stage. Even the 'formal-logical something' is not bound to theoretical experience, but is free. This principle applies also in regard to the atheoretical, religious, valuational, aesthetic comportment.

So if the formal-logical something cannot be motivated through a specific stage or level, a qualitatively different motivation must be found.

The something of formal-logical objectivity is not bound to something object-like. Fundamentally it leads back to the sense of the *experienceable as such*. Everything experienceable is *something*.

Not yet the ultimate motivational level of the 'something' but only in the sphere that is proper to it.

The experienceable [*Erlebbare*] as such, conceived as 'something', is already theoretized. Religious experience: the possibility, residing in experience as such, that it can be clothed in 'something', that everything experienceable contains the character of 'something'. In other words, *the character of 'something' belongs in an absolute way to life as such*: this is the phenomenological something. It extends to the sphere of life, in which nothing is yet differentiated, nothing is yet worldly: the phenomenological character of 'something' is pre-worldly. The primal character of 'something in general' is the basic character of life as such. Life is in itself motivated and tendential: motivating tendency, tending motivation.

163

The basic character of life is to live *toward* something in determinate experiential worlds. The mark of this is given in the 'something' .

This primal sense of the 'something' must be seen in pure phenomenological intuition. This is difficult, but despite objections it is necessary.

This pre-theoretical, pre-worldly 'something' is as such the grounding motive for the formal-logical 'something' of objectivity. The latter's universality is grounded in the universality of the pre-theoretical primal-something [*Ur-etwas*]. [219]

The Pre-theoretical Something		The Theoretical Something	
pre-worldly something	worldly something	objective formal-logical something	object-like something
(fundamental moment of life as such)	(fundamental moment of definite experiential spheres; aesthetic)	(motivated in the primal-something)	(motivated in the genuine experiential world)
primal-something	genuine experiential world		

Therefore: the theoretical 'something' exists only if the historical self [*historische Ich*] steps out of itself and enters into the process of de-vivification. Unavoidable condition of everything theoretical; if de-vivified, then concepts exist.

The experienced 'something' is not a concept but is *identical* with the motivational process of life as such and its tendency; therefore not a concept [*Begriff*], but a *recept* [*Rückgriff*].

Problem of the phenomenological concept, i.e. how to go back.

So, despite Natorp, there is an experience of experience, which is the understanding of experience from its motivation.

If one stands in a phenomenologically intuitive relation to life as such, to its motivation and tendency, then the possibility arises of understanding life as such. Then the *absolute comprehensibility* of life as such will emerge. Life as such is *not* irrational (which has nothing whatever to do with 'rationalism'!).

Phenomenological intuition is the experience of experience. The understanding of life is *hermeneutical* intuition (making intelligible, giving meaning).

The immanent historicity of life as such constitutes hermeneutical intuition. Once these insights are obtained, it emerges that the meaningfulness of language does *not* have to be theoretical.

[220] To the extent that meaningfulness is not as such theoretical there arises the possibility of phenomenological intuition, directed toward the *eidetic*, not toward generalizations. Since that which possesses meaning does not have to be theoretical, expressions of meaning are not tied to generalizations.

If one grasps the un-theoretical character of the meaningful, what follows is the possibility of a communicative science of phenomenology.

Aim of phenomenology: the investigation of life as such. Apparent suitability of this philosophy for worldview. The opposite is the case.

Phenomenological philosophy and worldview are opposed to one another.

Worldview: this is bringing to a standstill. (Natorp maintains this against phenomenology.) Life, as the history of the spirit in its transcendental expression, is objectivized and frozen in a definite moment. Religious, aesthetic, natural-scientific attitudes are absolutized. All philosophy of culture is worldview philosophy. It freezes definite situations in the history of the spirit and wants to *interpret culture*. Worldview is freezing, finality, end, system. Even Simmel in his last works does not grasp life as such, i.e. he grasps the transcendental historical rather than the absolute historical.

But *philosophy* can progress only through an absolute sinking into life as such, for *phenomenology* is never concluded, only *preliminary*, it always sinks itself into the preliminary.

The science of absolute honesty has no pretensions. It contains no chatter but only *evident steps*; theories do not struggle with one another here, but only genuine with ungenuine insights. The genuine insights, however, can only be arrived at through honest and uncompromising sinking into the genuineness of life as such, in the final event only through the genuineness of *personal life* as such.

Editor's Afterwords to the First and Second Editions

To the First Edition (1987)

In this volume the earliest extant lecture-courses of Martin Heidegger are published for the first time. They were held by the 29-year-old privatdocent at the University of Freiburg in 1919. The topic of the first lecture-course was changed from that previously announced in the register of courses. For the 'war emergency semester for war veterans', which lasted from 25 January till 16 April 1919, Heidegger had announced a two-hour course on Kant; instead, he gave a two-hour course on 'The Idea of Philosophy and the Problem of Worldview'. For the summer semester of 1919 he announced two one-hour lecture-courses, which he did in fact hold: 'Phenomenology and Transcendental Philosophy of Value' and 'On the Nature of the University and Academic Study'. As can be concluded from the dating of a transcript, the latter lectures were held at fortnightly intervals, the lectures of the other two courses on a weekly basis.

Available for this edition were Heidegger's handwritten manuscripts of the lecture-course from the war emergency semester as well as that for 'Phenomenology and Transcendental Philosophy of Value'. The manuscript for 'On the Nature of the University and Academic Study' is lost; an extensive search by Heidegger's literary executor, Dr Hermann Heidegger, was without result. For all three courses there are transcripts from Oskar Becker; two further transcripts, made by Franz-Josef Brecht, supplement Heidegger's manuscripts.

A thorough comparison of the lecture manuscripts with the transcripts shows that Heidegger [222] frequently diverges from the manuscript in his oral presentation, but did not vary the logical order of his thoughts. Here, therefore, the manuscripts of the lecture-courses are reproduced verbatim.

In order to compensate, at least partially, for the loss of the third lecture manuscript, the corresponding transcript from Oskar Becker, which is the only known document of this lecture-course, is included as Appendix I to the present edition.

The manuscript of the lecture-course on 'The Idea of Philosophy and the Problem of Worldview' comprises 67 paginated quarto sheets. The right-hand third of the pages leaves room for additions and extra remarks, usually related by insertion marks to the main text.

The manuscript of the lecture-course on 'Phenomenology and Trans-cendental Philosophy of Value' consists of 37 sheets: the Introduction ('Guiding Principles of the Lecture-Course') together with a supplement (here under the heading 'Aim of the Lecture-Course') which breaks off at the end of the sheet and whose continuation is not extant, as well as the continuous main text of 26 sheets. To this are added two short supplements, which are incorporated into the text in accordance with Heidegger's indications. A further 2-page supplement was found with the title 'Considerations on Negation'. With the help of the two transcripts this could be identified as the final chapter of the lecture-course. The manuscript of the main text breaks off abruptly with a marginal remark on the – here not named – criterion of negation: 'Rickert does not bother to ask about my right to use this phenomenon as a criterion. How do I know that it is valid?' (p. 150 [200]). The argumentative transition to Section 13 ('Considerations on Negation') could, through insertion of the two sections prior to this remark [223] ('Rickert does *not* . . . genu-ine?') be supplemented from the transcript of Franz-Josef Brecht.

The transcript of the lecture-course 'On the Nature of the University and Academic Study' comprises 19 consecutively numbered notebook pages. It bears Oskar Becker's handwritten title 'M. Heidegger: Excerpts from the Lecture-Course: On the Nature of the University and Academic Study (Summer Semester 1919 Freiburg)'. Its designation as 'excerpts' accords with the abrupt beginning in its course of thought and the absence of any introduction to the theme. The date with which Becker marks the first page of his transcript is 3.6.1919. According to the register of courses, however, the summer semester began on 26.4.1919; in any case, as can be gathered from the dating of Brecht's transcript of the course 'The Idea of Philosophy', Heidegger started this lecture-course on 9.5.1919. Becker probably did not attend the course on 'The Nature of the University' from the beginning. The dates of the further lectures as noted at the edge of Becker's transcript (17.6. and 1.7.1919) lead to the further conclusion that Heidegger gave this two-hour lecture-course at fortnightly intervals. The archive records of Freiburg University provide no further information on this.

For Heidegger's two lecture-manuscripts there were transcriptions from Hartmut Tietjen, which provided an essential basis for the editor's work. Collations of manuscript with transcription have allowed lacunae to be filled and errors to be corrected. The punctuation of the manuscripts has been greatly supplemented by the editor and orthographic errors have been corrected without notice. Underlinings (italicizations), also of proper names, follow the manuscripts.

The divisions and sub-headings were made by the editor. [224] In so far as they were indicated by Heidegger, sub-titles of the manuscripts have been adopted, or they have been formulated by the editor from a close reading of Heidegger's text. The overall title of the volume was also provided by the editor.

In many cases, notes and references to literature had to be completed and supplemented. In order that readability be impeded as little as possible, they have been put in footnotes, although many were also designated for oral presentation.

For valuable advice and help with the editorial work, thanks are due to Dr Hermann Heidegger, Professor Friedrich-Wilhelm von Hermann and Dr Hartmut Tietjen. I am also indebted to Martin Geszler for his thorough reading of the proofs. Special thanks to my wife Ute Heimbüchel, who was of inestimable help through many conversations and with the solution of numerous editorial and philological problems.

Bernd Heimbüchel
Köln, im März 1987

To the Second Edition (1999) [225]

Incorporated in this edition is an excerpt from Franz-Joseph Brecht's transcript of the last two lectures of the course from the 1919 War Emergency Semester. The excerpt relates to the material treated within the course 'The Idea of Philosophy and the Problem of Worldview' on pages 81–90 [106–17] of this volume. Its content rounds off the course by again taking up the main themes of the first lectures.

Franz-Joseph Brecht's transcript is the only one which covers the entire lecture-course from the War Emergency Semester. A transcript from Gerda Walther is incomplete, and from Oskar Becker there is only a 'Selection of the Most Important' from the two mentioned transcripts. Comparison with Brecht's transcript reveals that Becker's excerpt contains a number of misreadings.

Brecht's transcript was transcribed by Claudius Strube, and the excerpt printed in this volume was first published by him in *Heidegger Studies* 12 (1996), pp. 9–13.

Short Glossary

comportment: *Verhalten*
context of consciousness: *Bewußtseinszusammenhang*

determinateness: *Bestimmtheit*
de-vivification: *Entlebnis*
disclosure: *Erschließung*

environment: *Umwelt*
environmental experience: *Umwelterlebnis*
epistemology: *Erkenntnistheorie*
epistemological: *erkenntnistheoretische*
essence: *Wesen*
evaluation: *Beurteilung*
event: *Ereignis*
experience: *Erfahrung*

fact: *Tatsache*
factuality: *Tatsächlichkeit*

human sciences: *Geisteswissenschaften*

judgement: *Urteil*

lived experience: *Erlebnis*

material pre-givenness: *Materialvorgebung*

ought, the: *das Sollen*
ownness: *Eigenheit*

pregivenness: *Vorgebung*
pre-living: *Vorleben*
pre-worldly: *vorweltliche*
primal spring: *Ur-sprung*
primordial science: *Urwissenschaft*
process: *Vorgang*

science of value: *Wertwissenschaft*
spirit: *Geist*
subject-matter: *Sache*

thing-experience: *Dingerfahrung*

validity: *Geltung*
value: *Wert*

worldview: *Weltanschauung*
worldliness: *Welthaftigkeit*

Notes

I   Part One

Chapter One

1   Plato, *Sophist* (Burnet) 242 c 8 f.
2   Plato, *Republic* VII (Burnet), 533 c 7–d 4.

Chapter Two

1   Wilhelm Windelband, 'Kritische oder genetische Methode?' (1883), in: *Präludien. Aufsätze zur Philosophie und ihrer Geschichte*, 5th expanded edition, Tübingen 1915, Vol. II, p. 108.
2   Ibid. p. 109.
3   Cf. Heinrich Rickert, *Der Gegenstand der Erkenntnis. Einführung in die Transzendentalphilosophie*, 3rd revised and expanded edition, Tübingen 1915, p. 449 ff. (Conclusion).
4   Windelband, 'Normen und Naturgesetze' (1882), in: *Präludien*, Vol. II, p. 69.
5   Ibid. p. 72.
6   Ibid. p. 73.
7   Hermann Lotze, *Logik. Drei Bücher vom Denken, vom Untersuchen and vom Erkennen*, Leipzig 1874, p. 11 f. (Introduction).
8   Windelband, *Präludien*, Vol. II, p. 131.
9   Rickert, *Gegenstand*, 3rd edn, p. 207.
10 Ibid. p. 439.
11 Ibid. p. 437.
12 Ibid. p. 442.
13 Ibid. p. 207 ff.

I   Part Two

Chapter One

1   Aristotle, *Metaphysics* A 2, 982 b 11 f.
2   Sophocles, *Antigone* V. 100 ff., in: *Sophoclis Tragoediae*, cum praefatione Guilelmi Dindorfii, Leipzig 1825, p. 172. German translation by Friedrich Hölderlin ('O Blik der Sonne, du schönster, der / Dem siebenthorigen Thebe / Seit langem scheint . . .') in *Sämtliche Werke und Briefe*, ed. F. Zinkernagel, Leipzig 1915, Vol. III, p. 374 f.

Chapter Two

1   Cf. Paul Natorp, *Allgemeine Psychologie nach kritischer Methode*, Book One, *Objekt und Methode der Psychologie*, Tübingen 1912.
2   Paul Natorp, *Die logischen Grundlagen der exakten Wissenschaften*, Leipzig and Berlin 1910, p. 331.

Chapter Three

1   Edmund Husserl, *Ideen zu einer reinen Phänomenologie und phänomenologischen Philosophie* [Book One = *Ideen* I], in *Jahrbuch für Philosophie und phänomenologische Forschung*, ed. E. Husserl, Halle an der Saale 1913, Vol. I, p. 150.
2   Ibid. p. 144.
3   Ibid. p. 145.
4   Ibid. p. 139.
5   Natorp, *Allgemeine Psychologie*, Vol. I, p. 190 f.
6   Ibid. p. 191.
7   Ibid. p. 189 f.
8   Nicolai Hartmann, 'Systematische Methode', in *Logos* III (1912), p. 137.
9   Cf. Natorp, 'Husserls *Ideen zu einer reinen Phänomenologie*', in *Logos* VII (1917/18), p. 236 ff.
10 Natorp, *Allgemeine Psychologie*, Vol. I, p. 191.
11 Ibid. p. 192.
12 Ibid.
13 Natorp, 'Bruno Bauchs *Immanuel Kant* und die Fortbildung des Systems des kritischen Idealismus', in *Kantstudien* XXII (1918), p. 437.
14 Cf. what was said above concerning critical idealism, p. 64 [82] f.
15 Natorp, *Allgemeine Psychologie*, Vol. I, p. 196.
16 Ibid. p. 193.
17 Ibid. p. 200.
18 Ibid. p. 211.

19 Ibid. p. 206.
20 Natorp, 'Bruno Bauch', p. 439.
21 Ibid. p. 440.
22 Natorp, *Allgemeine Psychologie*, Vol. I, p. 199.
23 Natorp, 'Husserls *Ideen*', p. 246.
24 Natorp, *Allgemeine Psychologie*, Vol. I, p. 192.
25 Natorp, 'Bruno Bauch', p. 434.
26 Ibid. p. 432.
27 Husserl, *Ideen*, Vol. I, p. 43.
28 Ibid. p. 44.

II   Part One

Introduction

1 To be conceived as problem of eidetic essence, meaning and content. Cf. Emil Lask, *Die Lehre vom Urteil*, Tübingen 1912, p. 118. In this way the problem of world and experience (the theoretical) and its genuine character are posed together! Phenomenon of signification in general.

2 Prior consideration of the Kantian transcendental philosophy and reference to the first Kantian expression of the problematic of transcendental philosophy; theory by way of theoretical problem (mathematical natural science).

3 Wilhelm Windelband, 'Kulturphilosophie und transzendentaler Idealismus' (1910), in: *Präludien. Aufsätze und Reden zur Philosophie und ihrer Geschichte*, 5th expanded edition, Tübingen 1915, Vol. II, p. 286 f.; Heinrich Rickert, *Zur Lehre von der Definition*, 2nd revised edition, Tübingen 1915; Heinrich Rickert, *Der Gegenstand der Erkenntnis*, 1st edition, Freiburg im Breisgau 1892.

4 Wilhelm Windelband, 'Geschichte und Naturwissenschaft' (Straßburg rectoral address, 1894), in: *Präludien*, Vol. II, pp. 136–160.

5 Edmund Husserl, *Logische Untersuchungen*, Vol. I, *Prolegomena zur reinen Logik*, 2nd revised edition, Halle 1913.

6 Emil Lask, *Die Logik der Philosophie und die Kategorienlehre*, Tübingen 1911; Emil Lask, *Die Lehre vom Urteil*, Tübingen 1912; Rickert, *Gegenstand*, 1st edition 1892, 2nd edition 1904, 3rd edition 1915.

7 Lask, *Logik*, p. 271 ff.

8 Richard Hönigswald, *Die Philosophie des Altertums*, Munich 1917.

9 The manuscript of the Introduction breaks off at this point [Ed.].

Chapter One

1 Wilhelm Windelband, 'Immanuel Kant. Zur Säkularfeier seiner Philosophie' (Lecture, 1881), in: *Präludien*, 5th edition, Vol. I, p. 145.
2 Johann Gottfried Herder, *Auch eine Philosophie der Geschichte zur Bildung der Menschheit*, in: *Sämtliche Werke*, ed. B. Suphan, Berlin 1891, Vol. 5, p. 509.
3 Hermann Lotze, *Mikrokosmos. Ideen zur Naturgeschichte und Geschichte. Versuch einer Anthropologie*, 2nd edition, Vols I–III, Leipzig 1869–1879.
4 Cf. ibid, Vol. I, p. 255.

Chapter Two

1 Wilhelm Windelband, *Über die Gewissheit der Erkenntnis*, Berlin 1873.
2 Hermann Cohen, *Kants Theorie der Erfahrung*, Berlin 1871; Wilhelm Dilthey, *Leben Schleiermachers*, Berlin 1870; Franz Brentano, *Psychologie vom empirischen Standpunkte*, Leipzig 1874.
3 Heinrich Rickert, 'Fichtes Atheismusstreit und die Kantische Philosophie', in: *Kantstudien* IV (1900), p. 166; cf. also the typical motto of this essay, p. 137: ' . . . here the point, the thought and the will are united in one, and bring harmony into my nature' (Fichte, 1798).
4 Hermann Lotze, *Logik*, Leipzig 1843, p. 7; cf. p. 9.
5 Windelband, *Gewissheit*, p. 54 n.
6 Ibid. p. 64.
7 Ibid. p. 68.
8 Windelband, 'Kant', *Präludien*, Vol. I, p. 139.
9 Ibid. p. 139 f.
10 Ibid. p. 142.
11 See my lectures on 'The Idea of Philosophy and the Problem of Worldview', p. 26 [31] ff. above.
12 Windelband, 'Was ist Philosophie? (Über Begriff und Geschichte der Philosophie)', 1882, in: *Präludien*, Vol. I, p. 26 ff.
13 Windelband seeks to overcome the problem of the holy and of philosophy of religion in his essay 'Das Heilige (Skizze zur Religionsphilosophie)', 1902, in: *Präludien*, Vol. II, pp. 295–332. On this see also Jonas Cohn, *Religion und Kulturwerte. Philosophische Vorträge*, published by the Kant-Gesellschaft, Vol. 6, Berlin 1914.
14 Paul Natorp, 'Hermann Cohens philosophische Leistung unter dem Gesichtspunkt des Systems', in: *Philosophische Vorträge*, published by the Kant-Gesellschaft, Vol. 21, Berlin 1918.
15 Windelband, 'Was ist Philosophie?', *Präludien*, Vol. I, p. 27 f.
16 Ibid. p. 29.
17 Ibid.

NOTES

18 Ibid, p. 32 n.
19 Christoph Sigwart, *Logik*, 4th revised edition, Tübingen 1911, Vol. I, p. 162 n.
20 Rickert, *Gegenstand*, 1st edition 1892, p. 50; 2nd edition 1904, p. 91.
21 Ibid. 3rd edition 1915, p. 172.
22 Windelband, 'Beiträge zur Lehre vom negativen Urteil', in: *Straßburger Abhandlungen zur Philosophie. Eduard Zeller zu seinem siebzigste Geburtstage*, Freiburg im Breisgau and Tübingen 1884, pp. 165–96; 'Vom System der Kategorien', in: *Philosophische Abhandlungen. Christoph Sigwart zu seinem siebzigsten Geburtstage*, Tübingen, Freiburg im Breisgau and Leipzig 1900, pp. 41–58.
23 Cf. also Windelband's essay 'Logik' in the Festschrift for Kuno Fischer: *Die Philosophie im Beginn des zwanzigsten Jahrhunderts*, ed. Windelband, 1st edition Heidelberg 1904, 2nd edition 1907, pp. 183–207. The later contributions in Arnold Ruge's *Encyclopädie der philosophischen Wissenschaften*, Vol. I, *Logik*, Tübingen 1912: 'Die Prinzipien der Logik', pp. 1–60, and in his 'Ein leitung in die Philosophie' (Tübingen 1914), to be mentioned later.
24 Windelband, 'Was ist Philosophie?', *Präludien*, Vol. I, p. 29.
25 Ibid. p. 30.
26 Ibid.
27 Ibid. p. 31
28 Ibid. p. 32.
29 Ibid. p. 31.
30 Ibid, p. 34.
31 Ibid. p. 37.
32 Ibid.
33 Ibid. p. 38.
34 Ibid. p. 39.
35 Ibid. p. 40.
36 Ibid. p. 42.
37 Ibid.
38 Ibid. p. 43.
39 Ibid.
40 Ibid. p. 44.
41 Ibid. p. 45.
42 Ibid. p. 46.
43 Ibid.
44 Windelband, 'Logik', Festschrift Fischer, p. 184.
45 Ibid. p. 189.
46 Windelband, 'Kategorien', Festschrift Sigwart.
47 Windelband, 'Negatives Urteil', Festschrift Zeller, p. 168.
48 Ibid. p. 169 f.

49 Ibid. p. 170.
50 Windelband, 'Was ist Philosophie?', *Präludien*, Vol. I, p. 34.
51 Windelband, 'Negatives Urteil', Festschrift Zeller, p. 173 f.
52 Ibid. p. 185 f.
53 Ibid. p. 187.
54 Ibid.
55 Ibid.
56 Ibid. p. 189 f.
57 Section 3, p. 140 ff.
58 Windelband, 'Kategorien', Festschrift Sigwart, p. 43.
59 Ibid. p. 43 f.
60 Ibid. p. 44.
61 Ibid. p. 44 f.
62 Ibid. p. 45 f.
63 cf. Windelband, 'Logik', Festschrift Fischer, p. 192.
64 Windelband, 'Kategorien', Festschrift Sigwart, p. 47.
65 Ibid.
66 Ibid. p. 48.
67 Ibid. p. 50. Cf. Hermann Lotze, *Logik, Drei Bücher vom Denken, vom Untersuchen und vom Erkennen* (1874), ed. G. Misch, Leipzig 1912, Book III, Ch. 4: 'Reale und formale Bedeutung des Logischen'.
68 Windelband, 'Logik', Festschrift Fischer, p. 195.
69 Wilhelm Dilthey, *Einleitung in die Geisteswissenschaften*, Vol. I, Leipzig 1883.
70 Ibid. p. 33.
71 Ibid. p. 40.
72 Ibid. p. 109; cf. p. 117.
73 Ibid. p. 40 f.
74 Ibid. p. 149.
75 Windelband, 'Geschichte und Naturwissenschaft', in *Präludien*, Vol. II, p. 142.
76 Ibid. p. 143.
77 Ibid. p. 143 f .
78 Ibid. p. 144.
79 cf. ibid. p. 148.
80 Ibid. p. 145.
81 Heinrich Rickert, *Wilhelm Windelband*, Tübingen 1915.

Chapter Three

1   Immanuel Kant, *Prolegomena zu einer jeden künftigen Metaphysik*, in: *Werke*, ed. E. Cassirer, Berlin 1913, Vol. IV, p. 44.
2   Heinrich Rickert, *Kulturwissenschaft und Naturwissenschaft*, 3rd edition, Tübingen 1915, p. 33.

3   Ibid. p. 34.
4   Ibid. p. 60.
5   Ibid. p. 90.
6   Ibid. p. 94 f.
7   Ibid. p. 97.
8   Ibid. p. 156.

II   Part Two

Critical Considerations

1   Rickert, *Gegendstand*, 3rd edition 1915, p. X.
2   Heinrich Rickert, 'Zwei Wege der Erkenntnistheorie', in: *Kantstudien* XIV (1909), pp. 169–228.
3   Richard Kroner, *Über logische und aesthetische Allgemeingultigkeit*, Leipzig 1908; Emil Lask, 'Gibt es einen Primat der praktischen Vernunft in der Logik?', in: *Bericht über den III. Internationalen Kongreß für Philosophie zu Heidelberg*, 1–5 September 1908, ed. Th. Elsenhans, Heidelberg 1909.
4   Rickert, *Gegenstand*, 3rd edition, p. XII.
5   Rickert, *Windelband*, p. 29.
6   Rickert, *Gegenstand*, 1st edition, p. 40.
7   Ibid. p. 41.
8   Ibid. p. 42.
9   Ibid. p. 43.
10   Ibid. p. 45.
11   Ibid. p. 47.
12   Ibid. p. 47 f.
13   Ibid. p. 55 f.
14   Ibid. p. 58 f.
15   Ibid. p. 63.
16   Ibid. p. 47.
17   Ibid.
18   Ibid.
19   Ibid. cf. 2nd edition, p. 88 f.
20   Ibid. p. 49.
21   Ibid. p. 51.
22   Ibid. p. 55.
23   Ibid. p. 58.
24   Ibid. p. 55 f.
25   Ibid. p. 56.
26   Ibid.

27 Ibid. p. 57.
28 Ibid. p. 56 f.
29 Ibid. p. 57 f.
30 Ibid. p. 60.
31 Ibid. p. 60 f.
32 Ibid. p. 62 f.
33 Rickert, *Gegendstand*, 2nd edition, p. 116.
34 Ibid. p. 118.
35 *Gegendstand*, 1st edition, p. 68.
36 Rickert, *Gegendstand*, 2nd edition, p. 126 f.
37 Rickert, *Gegendstand*, 1st edition, p. 70.
38 Ibid. p. 83 f.
39 Ibid. p. 91.
40 Psychology and meaning interpretation. Representation of the subjective way and Rickert's critique of its inadequacy. Cf. § 10 above, p. 137 [181] ff., and the remarks in *Gegenstand*.
41 Rickert, *Gegendstand*, 3rd edition, p. 254.
42 Ibid. p. 303.
43 Ibid. p. 273.
44 Ibid. p. 255.
45 Ibid. p. 254 f.
46 Ibid. p. 255 f.
47 Ibid. p. 256.
48 Ibid. p. 257.
49 Ibid. p. 258.
50 Ibid.
51 Ibid.
52 Ibid. p. 259.
53 Ibid. p. 264.
54 Ibid.
55 See the Editor's Afterword, p. 167 [222].
56 Cf. Rickert, *Gegenstand*, 3rd edition, Chapter 4: 'Sinn und Wert', pp. 264–355.

Index